More than
Meets the Eye
Wyoming Along Interstate 80

More than Meets the Eye

Wyoming Along Interstate 80

Mary Ann Trevathan

High Plains Press
Glendo, Wyoming

The photograph of the Ames Monument on the cover is used
with permission of the Wyoming State Museum.
Other cover photos are by the author.
All photographs in the text are by the author
except those which are credited
to other individuals or agencies.

Library of Congress Cataloging-in-Publication Data

Trevathan, Mary Ann
More than meets the eye: Wyoming along Interstate 80/
Mary Ann Trevathan.
p. cm.
ISBN: 0-931271-20-7 (paper)
1. Wyoming--Guidebooks.
2. Wyoming--Biography.
3. Interviews--Wyoming
4. Interstate 80--Guidebooks.
5. Automobile travel--Wyoming--Guidebooks
I. Title.
F759.3.T74   1993
917.8704'33--dc20
93-4245
CIP

HIGH PLAINS PRESS
539 CASSA ROAD
GLENDO, WYOMING 82213

Contents

Preface

"WE DROVE ALL THE WAY across Wyoming last summer. There's nothing there."

Usually people who say this have driven through Wyoming via Interstate 80. The disgruntled tourists I've talked with had two complaints.

•• *Monotony.* "Whenever we stay overnight along the Interstate, my husband swears they move our motel during the night so we have to drive over the same route the next day."

•• *Desolation.* "There's no trees. There's no people!"

The first time I traveled across Wyoming I didn't much like the drive either—not the way I do today. I wrote *More than Meets the Eye* to make traveling across southern Wyoming more fun, whether by car, bus, bicycle, or armchair. If you get bored with the Interstate you can take some alternate routes partway, including a national scenic byway.

If you stay on I-80, you can see archaeological digs, dinosaur fossils, wild horses, antelope, and a lot of other sights you can't find just anywhere. But you won't come upon many tourist traps: "No chicken feathers or tomahawks," to quote anthropologist Chuck Reher.

People give places life. *More than Meets the Eye* is mainly about Wyoming people who live and work along the Interstate: miners, ranchers, artists, activists, a race track owner, a geologist, a service station owner, lawmen, anthropologists, legislators—and historians.

Never have I known people so in love with history as those who live in Wyoming. And as former archivist Gene Gressley points out, history includes more than the Old West. Abe De Herrera's account of being a police officer in the sixties and seventies is history. So are Dick and Wilma Hardy's descriptions of life on their ranch, Keith Black's and Steve Kesy's recollections of coal mining in the eighties, and Dick Randall's analysis of problems facing the Red Desert today.

Trona miners Barbara Miller and Stan Owen and mine superintendent Herb Price are historical figures, as is state penitentiary warden Duane Shillinger, and Bill Young, owner of the world's largest wind turbine.

David Roberts, a journalist and native Wyomingite, once told me, "Wyoming's a liberal state, in that people expect you to hold strong opinions. They'll probably disagree with you, but they'll grant you the right to say what you think." People say what they think in *More than Meets the Eye*, without hedging and without rancor.

After relaying some general information about Wyoming, this book takes you west across the Interstate from Pine Bluffs to Evanston. You can read it in any order. If you're in a hurry and you're driving from sunrise to moonrise, scan the overviews en route and leave the interviews to read at your leisure. You don't have to be driving across Wyoming to appreciate what people in this book have to say. You don't have to leave home at all.

Chapter 1
Entering Wyoming

FOR YEARS THE SIGN at the border read, "Welcome to **BIG** Wyoming!"

Wyoming is ninth largest of all the states, about twice the size of Pennsylvania, but it has the smallest population. Only about 470,000 people live here, roughly five people per square mile. Wyoming has more pronghorn antelope than people.

One reason not many people live in this state is that the federal government owns nearly half the land. Wyoming was the first state or territory to have a national park (Yellowstone), the first to have a national forest (Shoshone), and the first to designate a national monument (Devils Tower). It contains seven national forests, eight hundred square miles of water, and eleven major mountain ranges.

Another reason so few people live in Wyoming is that it is high, dry, windy, and cold. Wyoming's mean elevation— 6,700 feet—is second only to Colorado's. The state's average annual rainfall is fourteen inches, but southwestern Wyoming gets less than seven inches of rain per year.

Temperatures of minus thirty degrees are common in Wyoming in winter; minus sixty-three degrees has been recorded. Of all the states, only Alaska is colder. Snow has fallen somewhere in Wyoming every month of the year. As historian Dudley Gardner noted, "Winter is not a season in Wyoming. It is a possibility on any given day."

Some people claim that Wyoming is so windy, babies are born at a tilt. They say snow never reaches the ground, it's all horizontal—it just blows around until it wears out. They swear that on the rare occasions that the wind stops blowing, everybody falls down. The strongest wind velocity ever recorded in the state was 115 miles per hour.

Wyoming has intensely blue skies, smog-free air, free-roaming wildlife, and, some say, the best drinking water anywhere. It is a place of spectacular beauty, but an appreciation for some of that beauty has to be acquired.

Long-time residents tell newcomers that one thing Wyoming has is plenty of sky. They say you can look farther and see less in Wyoming than anywhere else. Newcomers terrified at first by the "desolate" desert or prairies later learn that open space becomes addictive, a component of quality living; sensing the vastness of the landscape becomes a form of prayer.

Owen Wister wrote the best-selling cowboy novel, *The Virginian*, in Wyoming. Wyoming sometimes calls itself the Cowboy State, and University of Wyoming athletic teams carry the Cowboy name. Automobile license plates display bucking broncos. Throughout the state seventy rodeos take place each year.

But less than ten per cent of Wyoming's income comes from farming and ranching. Three-fifths of all Wyoming homesteads failed, and most of those which survived were incorporated into larger ranches. Less than five per cent of the land in the state has ever been plowed, and more than half is covered with sagebrush.

Consider that it takes an average of forty acres of land in Wyoming to support one cow and you can understand the vast acreages Wyoming cattlemen need to survive. Along the Interstate the ranchers' situation is complicated by the "checkerboard" land sections the federal government granted to Union Pacific when it built the transcontinental railroad. Union Pacific was given alternate square mile (640 acre) sections—including mineral rights—for twenty miles north and twenty miles south of the railroad tracks. Cattlemen couldn't afford to settle on the remaining checkerboard sections without being able to expand, so the federal government now leases out much of that land for grazing. Union Pacific has since sold off some of its land. Swan Land and Cattle Company (which later became the Wyoming Hereford Ranch) bought the largest amount—549,423 acres.

Mining is Wyoming's chief means of support, followed by tourism. Wyoming leads the nation in the production of trona (soda ash) and bentonite, is second in uranium and coal, and sixth in oil and natural gas. Wyoming's coal is low in sulfur, so industries can use it without installing as many scrubbers.

Because of its dependence on mineral development, Wyoming has a boom-bust economy, and some Wyomingites say the booms are always short-lived and the busts go on forever. After the OPEC oil embargo of 1973, workers came from throughout the United States to work in the oil and natural gas wells near Evanston and Wamsutter, the coal mines at Gillette, Point of Rocks, and Hanna, uranium mines at Shirley Basin, and trona mines near Green River.

Traditional Mormon ranch towns in western Wyoming were invaded by newcomers who didn't understand their cultures; by developers who set up mobile home parks, promised services they couldn't deliver, went bankrupt, and left. Populations of communities doubled. Long-time residents accustomed to going to the mountains without seeing another person all day found their space invaded by people they didn't know or trust. Small communities suffered traffic jams.

By the mid-eighties the boom had ended. Mobile homes bought at premium prices were now worth next to nothing. Some owners simply abandoned them and moved on to other states. Company housing no longer needed was shipped to college campuses, and whole neighborhoods disappeared overnight. Houses in coal mining towns which once sold for seventy thousand dollars were offered for fourteen thousand, with only retirees able to bid on them, since there was no work.

Traveling across the Interstate you can see some of the graveyards of the boom times: rows of trailer spaces, their hook-up poles standing like cemetery markers until the next energy crisis resurrects them.

In Wyoming climate is a great leveler. How people cope with natural forces matters more than title or academic degree. Even so, Wyomingites take pride in their public schools and libraries. During the mid-eighties a Gannett poll placed Wyoming's public schools first in the nation. Wyomingites rank second in the nation in average educational level achieved (grade 12.4), first in per capita use of libraries. Wyoming's 1992 Scholastic Aptitude Test scores averaged 462 on the verbal portion, 516 on the math, while nationwide scores averaged 423 and 476.

Anthropologists say human beings have lived in Wyoming for twenty thousand years and that the first residents crossed the Bering Strait from Asia and migrated south. Their descendants were American Indians: Shoshones in the west, Crows in the north, Cheyenne and Arapahos in southeast Wyoming. Today about six thousand Arapaho and Shoshone Indians share the Wind River Reservation in central Wyoming.

The earliest Euro-American settlers were mountain men who trapped beavers to provide hats for rich Europeans. A few mountain men may have roamed here in the 1700s, but from 1820 to 1840 the largest number came. Starting in 1825, trappers held annual rendezvous where they traded their pelts for supplies. By all accounts these rendezvous were drunken orgies. Tamed-down reenactments take place today. One of the largest is on Labor Day weekend at Fort Bridger, along Interstate 80. People dress in period costumes, barter goods, and compete in events such as the women's frying pan throw and the tomahawk toss.

Between 1840 and 1868 about a third of a million pioneers came through Wyoming on the Oregon and Overland trails, on their way to Utah, California and Oregon. The Overland Trail ran near Interstate 80, and you can still see the ruts today.

Some cattlemen settled in Wyoming as early as the 1860s, including some European cattle barons who laid claim to land and hired men to manage it. Homesteaders arrived following the first Homestead Act of 1862. Their needs and those of the stockmen ran at cross purposes, and the two groups clashed. Later sheepmen and cattlemen fought. Wyoming wasn't very democratic then; brute force usually won out.

F.V. Hayden, Clarence King, and Major John Wesley Powell all completed geological surveys in Wyoming, in which they inventoried the territory's resources. Hayden promoted the popular theory that the West offered endless opportunity and that "rain follows the plow." Rainfall would increase, Hayden and other scientists promised, if people cultivated the land and planted trees.

Powell countered that the West lacked water and that only a limited number of people should live there. Today's Western water specialists say Powell was right.

Wyoming's towns along Interstate 80 began as tent cities for workers on the transcontinental railroad. Union Pacific hired surveyors, graders, tie hacks, bridge gangs, tracklayers, track-ballasting crews, and train crews, as well as men to mine coal to fuel locomotives. Wherever possible, surveyors routed the train close to the richest coal deposits.

Often a town's early survival depended on Union Pacific's placing it on the main route and building a roundhouse and machine shop there. The railroad is not the major employer in Wyoming today that it once was. It closed down its coal mines in the fifties, when it switched to diesel-powered engines. AMTRAK pulled out of Wyoming in 1983 in favor of a more scenic Colorado route, but it returned in 1991.

Wyoming became a territory in 1868, the same year the transcontinental railroad came through, and it was awarded statehood in 1890.

One last word about Wyoming history. Wyoming's official title is "The Equality State," and its motto is "Equal Rights." It was the first territory or state to pass a law prohibiting "discrimination on account of sex," in 1869. It was the first to grant women the right to vote and hold office, and it appointed the first woman justice of the peace, first woman governor, and first women jurors. In 1992 about a fourth of Wyoming's state legislators were women. The League of Women Voters originated in Worland, and Wyoming ranks fourth in the nation in per capita membership.

The state seal celebrates Wyoming's progressive attitudes—sort of. It shows a woman in a long, flowing gown, an Equal Rights banner behind her, a cattleman at one side and a miner on the other. But—the woman is standing on a pedestal!

Chapter 2

Pine Bluffs

PINE BLUFFS, crossroads town
Population: 1,054   *Elevation:* 5,047
*Question: What do the letters B. P. signify?

Places to Visit

•• State information and rest area just off I-80, west of town.
•• University of Wyoming excavation site next to rest area.
•• Texas Trail museum, park, and monument, off Market Street between Second and Third streets.
•• Archaeological Education Center, Second and Elm Streets.
•• Roping Club practice Tuesdays, Thursdays, and Sundays. U.S. 30 and Beech Street.
•• Reher Park. Miniature golf, free swimming pool.

A Brief Background

As you look out at the bluffs surrounding the town, imagine how they appeared nine thousand years ago. People then, as now, looked across miles of prairie to the mountains. They camped here and provided themselves water, firewood, edible plants, and small game.

Within a couple of miles of town more than eight hundred stone circles are visible—stones which some anthropologists say held down the bottoms of tepees used by Plains Indians more than one hundred years ago. Anthropologists can tell the family size, group size, and social organization of people who camped here by examining these circles. They can also determine the kind of tepees they had, what direction they faced, what time of year they camped here and for how long.

The tepees you see in town were purchased by local business people and painted by high school art students. Townspeople gathered and prepared the poles.

During the 1800s Pine Bluffs was a watering place on the longhorn cattle drives from Texas. Six hundred thousand cattle passed through here in 1871 alone. During the 1880s more cattle were shipped via railroad from here than from any other place in the world. The Overland Trail also passed through Pine Bluffs.

Pine Bluffs is lower in elevation than other Wyoming towns along the Interstate. It is surrounded by tiny ranching communities—Carpenter, Egbert, Hillsdale, and Burns—and it once had the only movie theatre in the area.

Until the sixties each small town had its own school district. In 1955 Egbert had so few students, its high school basketball team had only four players. And they still won games.

Take time to see the giant generators and barbed wire display at the Texas Trail museum. Ask anthropologists at the excavation site to explain the many levels of civilization uncovered there. Tour the boarding house where Union Pacific employees once lived. Above all, enjoy the gentle, easy hospitality of Pine Bluffs that represents the West at its best.

ᕋ

*Answer: In archaeological displays B.P. means Before the Present.

About the Close-Ups

•• Chuck Reher grew up exploring the artifacts around Pine Bluffs. Now he is an anthropologist in charge of the High

Chuck Reher oversees a dig at an archaeological site in the hills ten miles from Pine Bluffs.

Plains Archaeology Project. You can take part in the research if you want to.

•• By sharing some of their own history, Dick and Wilma Hardy let us know what life has been like for farmers and ranchers in Laramie County.

Close-Up: CHUCK REHER

WHEN CHUCK REHER WAS growing up in Pine Bluffs, he used to roam the area searching for Indian artifacts. Now, as Director of the High Plains Archaeology Project and Professor at the University of Wyoming, Reher shares his knowledge and enthusiasm with visitors passing through.

"We're not a tourist trap, with tomahawks and chicken feathers," Reher said. "We're not in the tourist business—it just happens to be tourists that come by."

Tourists are welcome at the museum in town and at the excavation site next to the Interstate. "When people are working there, there's a lot to see, and we give guided tours," Reher said. "Our philosophy is we tell you more than you want to know. And if people are really interested, we tell them even more."

If you are really interested, you can look over workers' shoulders as they dig—or if you have a week or more to spare, you can work at the site. "There are a lot of possibilities, if volunteers want to come try it out," Reher said. "They just need to be negotiated.

"Nobody should get the idea they can come down and dig right away—not for a few days, anyway. Those things need to be prearranged. Get hold of us and check it out, and we'll see what's possible. It isn't that you have to be right out there flogging the hot weeds, either. You can work in the lab."

The lab is in the educational center at Second and Elm streets. "You can learn a lot there," Reher said. "We're very technical and flooded with information."

"People are always telling us to talk down to people: keep it simple, make it brief. We provide technical information. That way people can spend as much time as they want and take in as much as they want."

Admission to the site and to the educational center is free. That is as it should be, said Reher. "Once you go that commercialized route, the educational benefits go down, the authenticity. In a big or small way you begin to lose that educational philosophy. We want to focus on what's good for archaeology, for education—not, how we balance the budget."

Evidently, Laramie County residents agree. In 1991 they passed a sales tax increase which included 275,000 dollars to construct a museum over the Pine Bluffs excavation site. Once that building is in place, the site will remain open year-round. Until then it is open only from June through August.

The High Plains Archaeology Project sponsors field tours

Chuck Reher, director of the High Plains Archaeology Project, views material with Heather Hovde, a volunteer, and Judi Higgins, a field archaeologist.

for school children and teachers, nature walks, and college extension classes. It holds a summer field school for archaeology students.

The students work ten days on, four days off, and take turns cooking for the group, working in pairs. They camp in tents in the hills, shower at a community center in town, and cook at the Masonic Lodge.

Camping out is part of archaeology, Reher said. So is cooking for thirty or forty people. "Another part is getting along with people. It's an intense time—we put in long hours." They used to work dawn to dusk, but now they spend eight hours a day on-site, starting at eight A.M.

Reher used to camp all summer in a tepee. "It's the most comfortable tent there is," he said. "It's roomy, it withstands the wind, it's vented so it's cool in summer, and it's snug in cool weather." The trouble was, the tepee wasn't practical for all the paper work the project requires, so he spends the summer in a travel trailer now.

"We encourage students to bring large tents, and we'll help them put them up," Reher said. "We tell them to bring a cot, to bring a chair." Even so, some students make do with pup tents.

The High Plains Archaeology Project works on two excavation sites at a time: the main one near the Interstate and another in an outlying area. Reher expects they will remain at the main site for another ten years.

"Then as we gradually pull out, we'll leave behind these museum facilities and probably we'll have a tour guide program," he said. As the project grows, he expects fifty thousand people to visit the site each year.

From September to June, Reher teaches anthropology courses on the University of Wyoming campus at Laramie. He is director of the anthropology museum and is archaeologist for Arapaho and Shoshone Indians on the Wind River Reservation near Riverton. He has been working on developing the visitors' center at the Vore buffalo jump site near Sundance, Wyoming—a huge sinkhole used for four hundred years, where five Plains Indian tribes killed and butchered as many as twenty thousand animals. This will be the most spectacular archaeological site in Wyoming, Reher said—maybe even in the world.

But come summer, Reher returns to the High Plains Archaeology Project in his home town. "We're not the Smithsonian," said Reher. "But you can have an educational experience here, as intensive as you want it. And we're still building."

Close-Up: DICK AND WILMA HARDY

DICK AND WILMA HARDY LIVE halfway between Carpenter and Egbert, towns with populations of about one hundred each, in a house Dick's father built in 1925. Nearby stands a classic red barn which once housed Dick's museum, a red tile silo, and a well-tended flower garden. Dick and Wilma have always wanted to travel, but have been tied down. They have had a lot of fun anyway.

Dick's father homesteaded here in 1907 on 160 acres—a quarter section—not enough in this country, Dick said. He later acquired additional land. He settled a mile away from the nearest well, and far enough from Muddy Creek that cattlemen didn't try to scare him off, as they did some homesteaders.

As soon as his father could, he dug a well which flowed until the sixties, when it filled with sugar sand. Since he didn't own a horse, he walked thirty-five miles to the state office in Cheyenne to prove up his homestead.

Dick's mother came from Nebraska with her family to a homestead just four miles from Dick's father's. Her father hired Dick's father to build her family's home, which is still standing.

Dick's parents married in 1910. They lived their first fifteen years in a tarpaper shack, which they built on to when the children were born. That shack is also still standing.

Dick began his education in small country schools, including one which his parents built on their ranch. When the school district consolidated, he rode the bus into Carpenter. School buses weren't standardized then. One year he rode in a converted Model T truck; another year the school bus was a bread truck. He graduated from Carpenter High School in 1931, in a class of seven.

After his parents bought their first car, a 1915 model T Ford, they started an egg route to the Wyoming Hereford Ranch and into Cheyenne. They carried egg crates on the running board and sold fresh eggs door to door. The Governor's Mansion was part of their route, as were several restaurants and the state capitol.

Wilma and Dick Hardy live on a farm which Dick's parents homesteaded in 1907. Like many Wyoming people, they share a strong interest in the history of the West.

"All of us had brooder houses," Dick said. "They had stoves in them—first coal, then kerosene, then electric. We'd get three hundred to four hundred chicks at a time. They'd come through the mail, in boxes with holes in the top, about twenty-five in each section."

Fires were a common hazard. The Hardys' brooder house burned in 1928. Later, when electric power outages occurred, chicks froze to death.

Dick met Wilma in 1934, at a camp meeting at the Free Methodist Church in Greeley, Colorado. Wilma and her family had moved there from eastern Nebraska. Dick and Wilma caught a ride in the back of a pickup truck to another church meeting in Colorado Springs, and that night Dick hitchhiked to Manitou and climbed Pike's Peak. He watched the sunrise from 14,110 feet altitude.

"When he came back down his shoes looked like rockers," Wilma said. "He was a young Atlas—and he wanted everybody to know it."

Wilma was a ravishing brunette who played the guitar and had a soul-wrenching singing voice. Dick proposed to her that weekend. They married the following March, when Wilma was sixteen, Dick twenty-one, and settled on a farm they rented a few miles from his parents' homestead.

"We married March 20 because his baby chicks were coming in the next two weeks, and he wanted us to be settled," Wilma said. "He would have done a lot better with the chickens if I wasn't there. Boy, when one of them would die, I'd die with them. I was a city girl; I'd never been on a farm before.

"The night we were married and came home we had dirt three inches thick on the floor. It had been one of those windy days. The coyotes were howling. Here was this little two-room house, with kerosene lamps, no plumbing.... But the house did have hardwood floors."

They soon started buying their farm—160 acres for a thousand dollars—which they paid off partly in eggs and chickens. They invested in a herd of dairy cattle—Holsteins—and some Black Angus beef cattle. "We were always tied down," Wilma said. "Whenever we'd go somewhere we'd always have to get back in time to do the chores."

"This wasn't wheat country then, it was general farming," Dick said. "Everybody had their chickens and their hogs and their cows, and they tried to make a living that way. We were pretty self-sufficient, but there wasn't any money. But we did get to raise pinto beans for a cash crop."

During the thirties, clouds of dirt blew in. After farmers harvested their beans, the wind blew the soil and buried the fence rows.

"It was so bad during the thirties, you could buy a three- to four-hundred-pound sow for five dollars," Dick said. "We'd do that, and butcher it and make sausage and lard and peddle it in Cheyenne."

"There's only one time I left the farm, and that was in 1939," Dick said. "We moved down to Sugar Loaf, Colorado, and I worked in mines there for awhile—gold and tungsten. But still, nobody had any money. And Wilma didn't like it there, especially after one of the miners got killed."

The Hardys had three children by then, ages three, two, and eighteen months. They have raised five children in all.

They moved to Greeley. "I got a job as a carpenter there," Dick said.

"For a dollar a day," said Wilma, "and when you asked for more, you lost your job."

They returned to the ranch in 1941, and for a few months Dick worked in construction at Francis E. Warren Air Force Base in Cheyenne.

They planted trees on their ranch, for soil conservation. "We planted three thousand to begin with. Then we'd replace them when something happened to them," Wilma said.

They started growing wheat. But dry farming alone wouldn't support their family. "In those years you worked out in the wintertime a lot," Dick said. "Every winter I'd have to get a job, just to keep going."

"And borrow from the bank," added Wilma.

"I've worked in Pine Bluffs, I've worked in Cheyenne, I've picked corn around for people.... The last few years I painted houses."

At one time he share-cropped seven quarter sections in

addition to farming his own land. He set up a cow-calf operation, with Galloway bulls and Black Angus cows. He sold them in 1975, when the cattle business became unprofitable.

"It was the last good time to sell cattle," Wilma said. "That got us out of debt for the first time in our lives. And we haven't been in debt since."

In 1978 their son Glen offered to buy their farm for a fair market price, with the understanding that they could continue living there as long as they wanted. "It was kind and generous of him," Wilma said. "And it gave us a nest egg for the first time."

After Dick's parents died, Dick and Wilma moved to the old homestead. Glen retired from his job at the telephone company and moved with his wife, Marilyn, to Dick and Wilma's former home.

None of the Hardys' children has gone into farming. Dick and Wilma say they encouraged their children to leave the farm and pursue more lucrative careers.

They said some southeastern Wyoming farmers have sold out to a family who now runs a dairy farm on more than three hundred thousand acres. Growing wheat here is no longer profitable. "It was okay when it brought a good price, but now wheat's only two dollars and something a bushel," said Dick in 1991. "It costs more than that just to get it harvested."

For years Wilma sang in church choirs and with the Sweet Adelines in Cheyenne, but now she stays home most of the time. She calls Dick her Rock of Gibraltar.

Dick has always wanted to travel, but has always been tied down. So he reads. He treasures books, especially old leather-bound tomes about ancient civilizations. And he collects antiques.

In 1961 he set up a museum in his barn, with a display of horse-drawn machinery, old tools, and a kitchen, bedroom, and sitting room of a typical homestead. He furnished the rooms with antiques he refinished, including a loveseat and chair from the old opera house in Cheyenne and an organ from a Colorado dance hall. The museum was registered with the Wyoming State Archives and with the American Association of Museums. Schoolchildren and their teachers, civic groups, and even some Greyhound bus tours visited the barn-turned-museum.

Dick continues to earn respect as a local historian, but he had to give up the museum. The reason: Wyoming wind. He just couldn't keep the wind-driven dust off his displays.

Chapter 3
Cheyenne

CHEYENNE, Wyoming's capital and largest city
Population: 50,008   *Elevation 6,062*
*Question: What famous writer lived at the Wyoming Hereford Ranch while he wrote a bestselling novel?

Places to Visit—Free Admission

•• Wyoming Information Center, I-25 and College Drive (note Robert Russin sculpture) or Cheyenne Area Visitors Council, 301 West Sixteenth Street (note hitching posts).

•• State Capitol, Capitol Avenue and Twenty-Fourth Street. Tours in summer.

•• Wyoming State Museum and Art Gallery. Barrett Building, Central Avenue and Twenty-Fourth Street. (Restaurant downstairs.)

•• Union Pacific Depot, Capitol Avenue and Eighteenth Street. Depot was built in 1886 and is open to visitors but not in use.

•• Historic Governors' Mansion (1905-1976). 300 East Twenty-First Street.

•• Wyoming Game and Fish Visitors Center, Central Avenue at I-25. Wildlife exhibits, aquarium, information booths.

•• F. E. Warren Air Force Base, Randall Avenue and I-25. Tours Thursdays, 7:30 A.M.

•• For stamp collectors: National First Day Cover Museum,

Randall and Bent avenues. The only museum in the world dedicated to first day covers.

•• For picnicking:

• Holliday Park, East Lincolnway. The world's largest steam engine locomotive, used until 1956, is on display here.

• Lion's Park, Carey and Eighth avenues across from Frontier Park. Swimming pool, lake, botanic gardens, miniature golf, recreation building. Ice skating in winter.

Places to Visit—Small Fee

•• Cheyenne Frontier Days Old West Museum, Frontier Park, Eighth and Carey avenues. Western Wagons, Frontier Days memorabilia. Recommended: Video showing dramatic moments from rodeos.

•• F. E. Warren Air Force Base Museum. History of Fort D.A. Russell in late 1800s. Call base (307-775-2980) for hours.

•• City Historical Tour (summers) via trolley. Two hours. Some tours include air force base, others Wyoming Hereford Ranch. Check in advance at Visitors Council if you have a preference.

•• Historic Downtown Walking Tour for those with special interest in Cheyenne's buildings. You buy informational booklet, tour by yourself.

A Brief Background

Cheyenne was named for the Cheyenne Indians. In Sioux language the name meant "people of a foreign language."

General Grenville Dodge laid out the city in 1867 as a construction camp for the railroad. Dodge noted that the four-square mile area contained twelve trees.

At first Cheyenne was largely a tent city; even the city jail was a tent. The city council didn't expect Cheyenne to last after the railroad completed construction here. The council issued business licenses for three months, rather than for a year.

Cheyenne remained an end-of-the-tracks town for six months, longer than any other Wyoming Union Pacific town. Its survival was assured when Union Pacific placed a round-house and machine shop here and built a branch line to Denver.

Fort D.A. Russell was established here in 1867 to protect the railroad. Its successor, Francis E. Warren Air Force Base, is a site for U.S. intercontinental ballistic missiles and is home of the "Peacekeepers."

Fires and crime plagued Cheyenne during its first years. In 1868 Cheyenne had seventy saloons and two churches, Roman Catholic and Episcopalian. Of its six thousand residents, about four hundred were women, two hundred children.

Cheyenne grew so fast, it became known as "Magic City of the Plains." When gold was discovered in the Black Hills during the 1870s, stagecoaches left three times a day from Sixteenth Street and Capitol Avenue for Deadwood, South Dakota. The trip took three days.

Cheyenne became the first town in the world to be lighted with incandescent lights, in 1882, and the first in the United States to have a county library, in 1886. In 1920 it became one of fourteen stops on the transcontinental airmail route. Its municipal airport then was one of the best equipped in the nation. United Airlines trained its stewardesses (flight attendants) here. United Airlines stopped flying into Cheyenne several years ago.

The Wyoming Hereford Ranch, just off I-80, five miles east of Cheyenne, is the oldest continually operating Hereford cattle ranch in the United States. It was founded in 1883 by Alexander Hamilton Swan and was part of the Swan Land and Cattle Company.

At one time the ranch extended south into Colorado, north fifty miles to Chugwater, and 175 miles east into Nebraska.

One hundred families lived and worked here. During the thirties it was reduced to sixty thousand acres. Dairy cattle— Holsteins—were raised in addition to Herefords. The ranch has changed hands eight times. Husky Oil and Quaker Oats corporations were previous owners. The current owners—an anesthesiologist, his wife, and their six children—are the first owners to live on the ranch.

The Hereford Ranch includes only eight thousand acres now, and 350 cattle. It employs three people year-round plus five summer workers. It is strictly a breeding operation, and cattle are sold by private treaty rather than by public auction. The former sale barn is sometimes rented out for wedding receptions or picnics.

Near the barn, monuments stand to two prize breeding bulls: Prince Domino (1914-1930) and Lerch (1976-1986). The owners paid 261,000 dollars for Lerch when they bought the ranch in 1978.

Cheyenne became Wyoming's territorial capital in 1886 and state capital in 1890. The state's part-time legislature meets forty days in general session during odd-numbered years and twenty days in budget session on even-numbered years. The general session convenes on the second Tuesday in January, the budget session on the second Tuesday in February. Committees usually meet during summer and fall, but members are reimbursed only travel expenses for those meetings.

Wyomingites expect their government officials to be accessible and accountable. Grounds to the Governor's Mansion are open to public tours, and the Governor drives his own car and lists his home number in the public telephone book.

Cheyenne's Frontier Days began in 1897 as a means of boosting local economy after a disastrous blizzard. Its founders were inspired by Greeley, Colorado's Potato Day. Two thousand people attended Frontier Day the first year. The top cowboy was awarded twenty-five dollars, the top horse one hundred dollars.

For years Charlie Irwin, subject of Anna Lee Waldo's book *Prairie*, managed Frontier Days. You can see his former home at 402 Twenty-Eighth Street on the corner of Pioneer. His brand is embedded in the sidewalk out front. Irwin's ranch was at Albin, northeast of Cheyenne.

Several successful ranchers, including some British ones, owned homes in Cheyenne. Carey Avenue was once called Millionaire's Row. Many of the homes were built from brick, and Cheyenne used to have its own brick factory.

Cheyenne has the only synagogue in Wyoming, at 2610 Pioneer Avenue. Its services are Conservative. About sixty people who follow the Jewish religion live in Cheyenne, about two hundred in all of Wyoming. Eleven Cheyenne Orthodox Jewish families keep kosher, although they have to travel to Denver to buy their meat.

During the early 1900s Jewish settlers homesteaded in at least a half-dozen sites north of Cheyenne. The largest community was at Huntley, near Torrington, where fifty-six Jewish families eventually homesteaded. They dug their homes in the sides of hills and carried water from a creek three miles away.

Miraculously, most of them remained on their land for at least five years, long enough to prove up their homesteads, sell them and move on. Some became successful business people in Cheyenne. The Homesteaders Museum, between Huntley and Torrington on Highway 85, has photographs and land records of these and other homesteads.

෴

*Answer: James Michener lived at the Wyoming Hereford Ranch while he was writing *Centennial*. He referred to the ranch in the book, but by a different name.

About the Close Ups

•• Democratic senator Lisa Kinney and former Republican representative Mary Ellen Crowley tell what it's like to serve in the Wyoming State Legislature.

•• David Johansen tells you everything you need to know about Cheyenne's Frontier Days. He is executive director.

•• At 96 Bessie Rayor recalls a lifetime of struggle—from steerage to landed wealth.

Close-Up: LISA KINNEY

IN 1991 LISA KINNEY was completing her second four-year term as Democratic state senator from Albany County, and she hadn't decided whether she would run again. (She did run in the fall of 1992 and won.) Kinney, an attorney, is married and the mother of three young children.

"It's very expensive to be in the legislature," said Kinney. "My law practice suffers when I'm gone. I sponsored a bill this past session that was very unpopular. My idea was to raise the salary so more people could afford to be in the legislature. What I fear is that eventually nobody will run except the very wealthy and people with special interests.

"My bill wouldn't have taken effect for four years, until after I was out. It was killed early on without even getting discussion on the floor. People just get this knee-jerk reaction to raising our pay."

Wyoming state legislators receive seventy-five dollars for each day they convene, plus a daily expense account of sixty dollars. They usually meet five days a week, for a total of forty days during odd-numbered years and twenty days during even-numbered ones. Kinney's bill would have raised the daily wage to one hundred twenty-five dollars and the per diem to seventy-five. The 1994 legislature will receive those amounts, under an amendment to that session's budget bill.

Lisa Kinney is a state senator, a lawyer, a former librarian, and a mother. She believes serving in the legislature is a public service which involves a great deal of time and energy.

But there is no guarantee the raise will be carried over to future sessions.

"People have a certain viewpoint that the legislature is not public service. It is public service. It's donating a great deal of time and energy to making things better for the state.

"It's not a career position, it's a volunteer position. It's fascinating and fun and I think everyone should do it—or at least serve on a school board or on a county commission. But I'm definitely in favor of shorter terms and letting as many people go through the process as possible, so they have an understanding as to what goes on.

"The years I've been in the legislature, it's been real serious. I guess they used to do a lot of partying. We get up at five or five-thirty and work before the committees meet at eight A.M. The general session starts at ten and goes on until late afternoon. Then there's a reception or dinner, and after that you work until you drop. It's not a lot of glory.

"I'm on three committees—judiciary, education, and health. Most committees start meeting in June. I average two days a month attending committee meetings when the legislature isn't in session.

"Then there's the reading we need to do, and letters to answer from our constituents. We have no budget for postage or photocopying or for secretarial help. We do all our own typing, all our own letter writing. There's too much work, too much to read, the issues are too complex, and we need help.

"My husband says I serve as a conscience to keep things on track—to bring up the minority viewpoint, the unpopular viewpoint, that will get people in trouble with their constituencies. Re-election is never a motivation for me. People will call up and say. 'If you do this, I'll make sure you never get elected again,' and I'll say, 'That's fine.' If people vote me out, that's okay.

"In some ways I do like being a woman in the Senate, and a relatively younger woman. We have lots and lots of school children coming through. It's real satisfying to know they can look down from the gallery and see not just older men. I'm glad my body is there to give the little girls the idea that they can be in the Senate too.

"You can find satisfaction in such little things. The bills that I've sponsored—they might affect just a few people. When I find one or two people injured by a law, why not correct it, especially if it's easy to do? Since I'm in the minority party, some of the ideas that I've generated don't have my name on them. I generally go by the philosophy that as long as you don't need to get credit for something, you can get a tremendous amount done."

One law Kinney takes pride in created an intermediate care facility for people in a state institution, so that "the quality of life for a few developmentally delayed individuals has been improved."

About a fourth of Wyoming State Legislators are women, but only four of those are in the thirty-member Senate. "It's hard to be a woman in the Senate. You can't take years of habit away from men who have grown accustomed to making decisions for women. We can't go into the steam room with them and talk about our favorite bills. We're under-represented. There's not enough of us women even to be a voting bloc.

"Information is power there. If you have a lot of information and can back it up, you can have a lot of persuasion. But if everything else is equal, it's male over female, Republican over Democrat.

"I get lots and lots of mail, but I wish I'd get more. We're supposed to be representing what our constituents want. If you only get five or six letters, that's a lot of letters in some cases. One hurdred to one hundred fifty would be more challenging. People do call—but I'm not sure that's the most effective way. We have a hot line where you can vote yes or no to a certain piece of legislation. I think a letter is better. You have to respond to a letter.

"If I were to serve another term I'd work on health insurance. Health insurance is the biggest problem in the state, and we just skirt around it. Insurance companies are exempt from anti-trust laws, so companies decide what geographical regions they want to cover, and they price-fix. Wyoming, Rhode Island, West Virginia and other small states are at the mercy of the insurance industry.

"Our legislature acts so cautiously—we don't want to make the insurance companies mad. Last year we didn't even have an insurance committee meeting until December. It's like milk toast insurance regulatory laws. If we do take a strong stand, the insurance companies could all get together and pull out. And I think that's okay too. We need to make changes nationally.

"One neat thing about the legislature—for the most part, legislators don't fight with each other and don't hold grudges. You have three hundred, four hundred, five hundred bills to vote on, and coalitions change all the time. People can disagree fervently, and at the same time, not hold their opinions against each other.

"A lot of people do look up to legislators. The people I've run across are uniformly hard-working and well-intentioned, and there's a reason they're elected. I just love it when I'm there. It's indescribably neat to put something into effect that can change the rules that society lives by. If I were in the majority party I could get a lot more done.

"People have entrusted a strong responsibility with me, and I feel I have to do something for them. I feel a lot of pressure, but I don't feel personally important. People call you 'Honorable.' When people call me Honorable, I say, 'Call me Hon. I feel more comfortable as "Hon" than as an Honorable."

Close-Up: MARY ELLEN CROWLEY

ELLEN CROWLEY WAS ELECTED to the Wyoming State Legislature in 1973, as Republican representative from Laramie County. She served six terms in all.

"When I was a freshman legislator I didn't know anything," said Crowley. "I don't know why I ran; I didn't know any procedures. The League of Women Voters used to sit in the balcony, and they evaluated the various members of the

Ellen Cowley, who served six terms in the Wyoming legislature, tells what it was like to serve in the "old days."

legislature. I was voted the one who improved the most my first year—because when I started, I didn't know anything!

"There were nine of us from Laramie County. Where I sat, I was surrounded by Fremont County people, and they were good to me. They adopted me. And Natrona County was good to me. Alan Simpson was in the house at that time, and Malcolm Wallop. There were statesmen in those days."

Crowley may not have known legislative procedures, but she came with good credentials. She had been Wyoming State Librarian, Assistant Attorney-General, and Law Clerk to U.S. District Judge Ewing T. Kerr. Crowley was the first woman to be appointed to the Attorney General's office in

Wyoming and the first Wyoming woman to be named law clerk to a federal judge.

"I've been given every break that could ever be given to anybody," Crowley said. "What I am most proud of is that I finally became the chairman of the Judiciary Committee. My freshman year I couldn't even get on it! We did great things in that committee, lots of recodifications of laws.

"Another thing I was proud of—we enacted a law that provided that no doctor or hospital could be sued before the claim was first presented to a pre-trial screening panel. Lots of times it could be settled out of court, before it hit the newspapers. But the Wyoming Supreme Court held the law unconstitutional. It's too bad, because it was modeled after the Montana law, and the Montana Supreme Court found their law constitutional.

"I worked very hard on the Child Abuse and Protection Act and the Adult Protection Act. For the child abuse law, we had meetings every morning at seven. The Director of the Health and Welfare Department drove down every morning from Wheatland [seventy miles], and representatives from the League of Women Voters and the American Association of University Women and a social worker for DePaul Hospital came.

"One of our committee members, a man from LaGrange, didn't like the bill. Those women from League of Women Voters and AAUW got on the phone to people in the LaGrange and Torrington area and told them to get after that guy. The bill passed, and I attribute it to those educated and interested people.

"We used to meet for forty days during the legislative sessions. We used to say we met forty days and eighty nights, because you would work like a dog. The Colorado legislature meets for six months, but they go home every weekend and take holidays! When you know these bills have to be taken care of, you work really hard.

"The Judiciary Committee would have about five hundred bills to consider—about a third of all the bills that were introduced. I had a policy to consider every single bill that was addressed to our committee. We didn't put out every bill, but we considered every bill.

"In the old days, the legislators used to just sit down and write out their bills. You get people who are unlearned in the law, and they can't write law. One bill I was assigned to 'clean up' covered a whole page. It was all one sentence, and it had no verb! Now writing legislation is very refined. Legislative Service Offices has good lawyers, and they appoint their best lawyer to the Judiciary Committee. The computer helps out a lot, too.

"In the old days, there was a lot of drinking. The Hitching Post bar was just filled with legislators, and a lot of lobbying went on there. There was a lot of drinking the last night, too, while we were waiting for bills to come down. But the last couple of sessions I was there, there wasn't much drinking at all. The Hitching Post even said they lost money on the legislators.

"Before word processors, when all the bills had to be typed, with no errors, no erasures, the secretaries really had a rough time that last night. Sometimes they collapsed at the typewriter. We would have to stop the clock so we wouldn't go over our forty days. We'd go to our rooms at four A.M. and sleep four hours, then come back at eight to finish up.

"We really had an interesting session with insurance. Insurance companies were pulling out and not insuring doctors. Mike Sullivan, who is now our governor, was a practicing lawyer in Casper, and he represented the insurance companies. He was a good lawyer.

"One year we had a packet of ten or eleven insurance bills to consider, and we met at least once a week through the summer and fall. A lot of meetings were held in Casper because it's centrally located. Committee meetings take a lot of time. My law practice suffered.

"In the House of Representatives we had to run for re-election every two years. I never campaigned before the primaries. I figured if the Republicans didn't want me, I didn't want to run against Republicans and Democrats both. Right after the primaries in August I campaigned. After Labor Day we'd really hit the sidewalk. We'd go to the telephone building, the banks, the state office buildings.

"People kept telling me I had to get out and ring doorbells, so one Saturday morning I did. At the first house, a woman answered the door holding a baby, with a dirty diaper in hand. She wasn't the least bit interested in learning about Ellen Crowley. At the second house the woman was in the middle of making bread. And at the third house a man answered the door with a beer in hand—he was watching a ball game. So after that, I got in my car and drove home.

"The last year I was there, in 1987, there were a lot of new faces, and they were pretty young people. I think there comes a time when you're out of step with the younger generation. I'm not saying they're right, but there are more of them than there are seventy-five-year-olds. I guess I was just too conservative. There were misunderstandings between me and some of the new legislators and between the Speaker of the House and me. I wouldn't be effective anymore, so it was time to get out. I resigned before the term was over, at the end of the general session in March, so the new person could be appointed and become an incumbent for the budget session.

"The big thing I had trouble with—there were young lawyers and a couple of girls whose husbands were lawyers and a couple of way-out leftist people and some way-out rightist conservatives—they had to debate on everything! They'd talk all afternoon on one bill. That was disgusting. You can say what you want to without repeating yourself."

Crowley and her attorney husband, Tosh Suyematsu, live on a quarter section of land near Burns. Crowley is semi-retired, but she keeps informed on state news and becomes involved when she thinks state laws are not being observed.

"I thoroughly enjoyed law-making. I was good at it. I was good at drafting legislation and cleaning up legislation. None of it bored me," Crowley said.

Close-Up: CHEYENNE FRONTIER DAYS

"WHEN A FAMILY OF SIX IN Kansas City looks for someplace to go on vacation in their van, Cheyenne Frontier Days looks pretty attractive," said David Johansen, executive director.

The annual celebration, held the last full week in July, used to be known as a "hell-on-wheels" party, but in recent years Frontier Days has become a family event with reasonably priced entertainment.

In 1992 afternoon rodeo prices ranged from $7.50 to $11.50, night show prices from $9 to $13. Those who don't want to attend a rodeo or night show can pay the one-dollar grounds admission and enjoy free concerts, a carnival, an invitational Western art show at the Old West Museum, and some 250 commercial exhibits.

Some people come for the free events: a static air display at the Cheyenne airport featuring huge cargo planes and even a stealth bomber; a downtown parade from nine to eleven Tuesday, Thursday, and Saturday mornings; breakfast served by the Kiwanis Club on Monday, Wednesday, and Friday.

"The breakfast began as a civil defense exercise to determine how many people they could feed, and how quickly, in event of a national disaster," Johansen said. "It's a great place to meet people. You find people there from all over the world."

Between nine and eleven thousand people at a time come downtown for ham, pancakes with butter and syrup, and coffee or milk. They sit on hay bales and watch Southern Plains Indian dances or listen to bluegrass music played by such groups as Cheyenne's Chugwater Philharmonic Band.

Johansen estimates that between 300,000 and 350,000 people came to Cheyenne during 1990 Frontier Days. Parking can be a problem, but a greater concern is finding a place to stay. "It's becoming a major issue. We're always crying for more hotels during the month of July."

Many people make hotel reservations a year in advance. Commercial campgrounds are usually booked by spring. The Frontier Days staff refers visitors to Laramie, Fort Collins, and Greeley, some fifty miles away, for motels or campgrounds.

All rodeo and night show tickets are reserved seating, except for a small standing area in front, and the earlier you buy your ticket, the better the seating, Johansen said. Rodeos begin at 12:30. Occasionally night shows featuring top country/western entertainers sell out. Last-minute tickets may still be available, but at scalpers' prices.

Frontier Days rodeos, "the grandaddy of them all," offer a total of four hundred thousand dollars prize money for roping and riding events. In the wildest and final event of each rodeo, cowboys mount wild horses and race them around the track.

As of 1991, contestants paid 275 dollars for each event they entered. If they won big, they might come away with ten thousand dollars. "The prestige is what counts," Johansen said. "To win or place in Cheyenne is a thrill." The top winners, plus winners of the chuckwagon races, receive Frontier Days belt buckles. (Each night show opens with chuckwagon races and women's barrel racing.)

*David Johansen, executive director of Cheyenne Frontier Days,
makes sure "new and exciting mistakes" happen only once.*

Traveling the rodeo circuit can be expensive, especially if
contestants bring their horses. Some cowboys rent horses
from other contestants once they get to Cheyenne.

Contractors from Colorado and Texas provide rodeo
stock, including six hundred steers for roping and bulldog-
ging. Animal rights groups usually attend and protest the
rodeos. "We do everything within our abilities to ensure the
comfort and health of animals in the park," Johansen said.

A staff of nine works year-round, planning and promoting
Frontier Days. An additional fifty or sixty people are hired
during the celebration. The remaining two to three thousand
workers are volunteers, including a thousand from Francis E.
Warren Air Force Base. "Our job descriptions are to support
the volunteers," Johansen said. "We have volunteers from all
over the world."

People claim that Frontier Days always brings rain to Cheyenne. "We have given some consideration to asking farmers to subsidize Frontier Days," Johansen said. "Without Frontier Days they might suffer some long summer dry spells.

"We always hope for no rain. Usually it just rains for twenty to thirty minutes and then it stops. But not always. We've worked hard on park drainage, to keep the park as dry as possible. We've even toyed with the idea of buying some kind of weather insurance. In 1985 we had a flood the week after the show. A few years earlier we had a tornado later in the summer.

"We take special precautions to make sure we're ready for any type of disaster. We meet each year with the civil defense people, and the National Weather Service calls our security office once or twice a day to give a short-term forecast.

"Probably the coldest Frontier Days ever recorded was in 1990. The western apparel retail stores in Cheyenne completely sold out of winter clothing. And that was the year we had our second-largest crowds!

"As you get closer to the show, each year more of what you do is put out small fires that come up—like entertainers giving the impression that if there's an electrical storm or a lot of rain, they won't show up. And the challenge of making the volume of sound from the night show acceptable to everybody in the grandstand. Each year we make new and exciting mistakes. We try not to repeat them two years in a row."

Johansen has been attending Frontier Days since he was a student at Casper College, and he said it hasn't really changed very much. "People are just driving newer cars. We've found a combination of events that work, and we keep repeating them every year. People come for the parades, they come for the pancake breakfasts, they come to party. There's something to do in Cheyenne for nearly twenty-four hours a day. For ten days you never have to sleep."

•• For information on motels and campgrounds or on night show programs, Frontier Days has a toll-free number: 1-800-227-6336.

Rules for the Main Rodeo Events

Have you ever wondered how rodeo events are judged? Here are the rules for six main events, according to the 1988 Official Handbook of the Professional Rodeo Cowboys Association.

In bronc and bull riding, half of the contestant's score is determined by how well the bronc or bull bucks. Top bucking horses sell for fifteen thousand dollars or more, bulls for as much as twenty thousand dollars.

•• *Saddle Bronc Riding.* The rider starts with feet over the bronc's shoulders. A good eight-second ride includes long spur strokes with the rider's toes turned out. The spurring motion should synchronize with the rhythm of the horse's jumps. The rider's feet should be straight out in front when the bronc's front feet hit the ground. They should strike the back of the saddle, with rider's knees bent, when the horse lunges into the air.

•• *Bareback Riding.* A leather strap is secured around the horse, and the rider, who wears a glove, hangs onto the end of the strap. The rider must spur the horse, maintain control, and stay on for eight seconds.

•• *Bull Riding.* A flat braided rope is secured around the bull, and the gloved rider wraps the tail of the rope around his hand. The rider must stay on for eight seconds. No spurring is required.

•• *Calf Roping.* This event requires teamwork between rider and horse. The rider chases a calf, on horseback, and ropes the calf around the neck. The rider then dismounts, throws the calf to the ground, and ties any three of its legs. The calf must remain tied six seconds or the roper is disqualified.

•• *Steer Wrestling.* This requires two horses, two riders and one steer. The steer wrestler chases the steer on horseback. The assistant, a hazer, rides parallel and helps keep the steer running in a straight line.

The wrestler rides up alongside the steer and slides on top of it, arms around the steer's horns. The wrestler lifts up on the right horn and pushes the steer down with the left hand to gain the leverage to throw the steer.

•• *Team Roping.* The leading rider (the header) ropes the steer around both horns, or around the whole head, or around one horn and the whole head.

The heeler ropes both hind feet of the steer. When both ropers' horses are facing the steer and their ropes are taut, their time is complete.

Close-Up: BESSIE RAYOR

BESSIE RAYOR STANDS BARELY five feet tall, but she is an imposing presence, energetic and decisive. She looks to be in her sixties but, in 1991, she was actually ninety-six. She is a woman of means—a street in Cheyenne carries her name— and she earned every penny the hard way. This is her story.

She was born near Odessa, Russia, during the 1890s. Some of the worst pogroms happened there, especially during Passover, a time of open season on Jews. Her parents were involved in an underground movement helping Jews escape to Romania.

Bessie moved to the United States when she was fourteen years old. Her mother had died, and a cousin visiting from Indiana offered to bring Bessie home to Fort Wayne with her. Her father sent her to America with a bag filled with gold pieces, which she wore around her neck. He booked first-class passage for her three-week journey across the Atlantic from Hamburg, but her cousin changed Bessie's ticket to steerage and kept the first-class ticket for herself.

Steerage was a dark, dank cellar where men, women, and children were crowded together in narrow wooden bunks. Seasickness was universal. Sometimes hundreds of people would be vomiting at the same time. By the end of the journey everybody in steerage, including Bessie, had acquired a headful of lice.

They landed at Ellis Island, where they were showered, disinfected, and examined by immigration officials to determine whether they were healthy. Anyone who failed inspection was sent back to the homeland. Bessie passed. But now she faced another hurdle. Her cousin, who had debarked much earlier, went on to Indiana without her, even though she knew Bessie couldn't speak English. The Hebrew Immigrant Society helped her board a train for Fort Wayne. After riding for three days, she arrived at her aunt's home in the middle of the night.

Her aunt took Bessie's bag of gold and kept it, in payment for her room and board. She enrolled Bessie in school for three months, then put her to work in her grocery store. Any more schooling would be a waste, her aunt said. "You'll get married soon. You don't need it."

Bessie protested, to no avail. She confided in a teacher, who sent her to the Young Women's Christian Association. Over her aunt's strong objection—she was sure Bessie would be converted to Christianity—Bessie moved into the YWCA, continued her schooling, and worked part-time in the cafeteria to pay her room and board. The aunt kept Bessie's clothes, in protest.

Bessie moved to Chicago and found a job in a publishing house. "It never entered my mind how I was going to live," she said. "I was secure. I felt I could do it."

She fell in love with Bernard Leon Rayor, an army recruit from Denver. He was soon shipped out, but after the war

Bessie Rayor, now a woman of means, once went door to door with her two babies asking for a place to spend the night.

(World War I) he returned to Chicago and married Bessie. They moved to Denver, where he tried selling electric generators without much success.

Within a year their first baby was born, at a neighbor's home, because they had no money to go to a hospital. They moved to Cheyenne, where Bernard found a job reading meters. A year later they had two babies, and no home. "We stayed one night in a hotel. Then I went from door to door with my two babies, crying, 'I need a place!'" A sympathetic woman allowed the family of four to sleep in her kitchen until they could afford to rent an unfinished garage.

The garage had no running water and was cold—so cold, the stove would ice over. Not until after their fourth child was born did they live in a house with running water. They had five babies in all. "I wasn't a bit afraid, and I wanted those children." Their third child died when he was four days old.

"I had to scheme how to have food, how to do things. I wanted eggs. I couldn't afford eggs—but cracked eggs I could afford." She wanted a chicken. She couldn't afford a chicken, but she bought an old rooster and butchered it herself. "I was strong. I could see the future. I was never afraid."

They saved enough from Bernard's salary for a down payment on a house. For six years they augmented their income by buying run-down houses, moving into them, fixing them up and selling them—thirteen houses in all. Then in 1926, Bessie noticed a vacant office in downtown Cheyenne and on impulse, rented it, thus launching their full-time career in real estate.

They bought land cheap, east of Cheyenne on the other side of a hill, speculating that eventually that area would become a residential center. "I knew that some day that hill would have to come down." They built homes, sometimes letting people meet their down payments by doing the finishing work themselves. Even during the Depression, they never foreclosed on anyone.

In 1936, just as they were getting established financially, Bernard became seriously ill, and Bessie realized she would have to be the sole support of the family. "I was very strong, very powerful. I was never sick. I'd make a living." The only way she knew to work without leaving her children was to run a tourist camp, the forerunner of a motel. So she had one built. She borrowed money to buy land and bought lumber on credit.

She started with ten units. When they were completed she couldn't make payroll, so she went to the Jewish business community for help. They turned her down. "Finally a friend of my husband offered me ten thousand dollars, with no note.

I personally came and paid all the workers the full amount. They were crossing themselves!"

She bought furniture damaged in transit, purchased linens on credit, and opened what is now the Cheyenne Motel. As soon as she started making a profit, banks lent her money. She built more houses and purchased an apartment building and two additional motels—Twin Chimneys and the Scott Motel, where Hardee's Restaurant now stands. She financed her investments by keeping the Cheyenne Motel continually mortgaged. "I didn't do little deals. I didn't stop at anything. I borrowed money, I paid it back."

If she were a man, she said, she would have become a millionaire. "In those days they didn't have women who could do business." When her children were grown she set each up in business. Later she helped her grandchildren through college.

Bernard died in 1959. Bessie moved to Miami Beach and went back to school, taking classes in English, typing, general science, modern math, astronomy, child psychology, gourmet cooking, and the philosophy of Spinoza. She remarried, becoming Mrs. Isador Berger. Widowed again and in her mid-eighties, she moved back to Cheyenne.

Still healthy and confident, she takes her financial success for granted. "I was very strong, very powerful. I could see the future. I was never afraid.

"It's the truth, what I tell you."

✢

Chapter 4
Cheyenne to Laramie

*Question: What does Vedauwoo mean?

A Brief Background

When you leave Cheyenne, you can take either I-80 or Happy Jack Road west toward Laramie. Happy Jack Road (named for Jack Hollingsworth, who hauled wood for the Union Pacific and laughed a lot) is a good two-lane paved road leading to Curt Gowdy State Park twenty-four miles west of Cheyenne. (Curt Gowdy, the sportscaster, grew up in Cheyenne.) The park has two reservoirs—for fishing and boating, not swimming—picnic areas, a sewage dump for RVs, and reasonably-priced campsites which sometimes sell out on summer weekends. The road continues another fourteen miles before rejoining Interstate 80 at the highway summit.

Via the Interstate, Laramie is forty-nine miles from Cheyenne. You'll travel from prairie to mountain country. It may seem as though the countryside along the way is isolated, but there is a public school just off the Interstate on Harriman Road, about eighteen miles west of Cheyenne. As of 1991 twenty-three children were enrolled, in kindergarten through sixth grade. Two teachers and an aide are employed there.

About twenty-five miles west of Cheyenne, the Remount turnoff leads to the ranch where Mary O'Hara lived and wrote

"Crystal Castle," near Buford, is the only house in Wyoming made of formaldehyde bottles gathered from mortuaries.

My Friend Flicka, Green Grass of Wyoming, Thunderhead, and other novels. (A Florida public school board recently banned *My Friend Flicka* because a character in the book says "damn" and calls a female dog a "bitch.") Mary O'Hara is the author's maiden name. University of Wyoming Archives has her personal papers under her married name, Struve-Vasa. Remount Ranch is no longer owned by Struve-Vasa family members, and it is not open to the public.

Short on gasoline? Lonetree Junction, at Buford, has the only gasoline station between Cheyenne and Laramie. You'll find a public telephone there and a post office, too, more than one hundred years old.

You can see why the place is named Lonetree because just ahead, a lone tree with a fence around it grows out of a rock. The Union Pacific railroad used to go by here, and engineers stopped and watered the tree. Local residents tell newcomers the tree is fenced because it is the only one in Wyoming.

Wyoming has a lot of log houses, but only one private residence constructed of formaldehyde bottles gathered from mortuaries. It is about three and a half miles north of the Interstate and is sometimes called the "Crystal Castle."

Do you enjoy solitude? Take exit 329 south to Ames Monument. It is just minutes off the highway, but it seems eons away. The town of Sherman once existed here. The monument is a granite pyramid sixty feet high, commissioned in 1882 by Union Pacific. Henry Hobson Richardson, nineteenth-century architect, designed the pyramid, and the sandstone medallions of the Ames brothers were sculpted by artist Augustus Saint-Gaudens.

The monument honors Oakes and Oliver Ames, Eastern shovel and tool manufacturers, who raised money to build the transcontinental railroad after Union Pacific ran out of funds. The brothers were later censored by Congress for their greedy and unethical profit-taking. The railroad used to pass just north of here, and this was the highest elevation on the original route: 8,247 feet. Railroad engineers used to stop here and check their brakes. The railroad was rerouted in 1901.

About three miles north of the freeway, over a gravel road, is the Vedauwoo (pronounced veé-da-voo) Recreation Area in Medicine Bow National Forest. Granite boulders nearly one and a half billion years old form grotesque configurations and impart a mystical spirit. The area is popular for rock climbing, picnicking, snowmobiling, and camping.

Travelers sometimes wonder why a bronze bust of Abraham Lincoln sits at the summit of Interstate 80. It was built by Robert Russin to commemorate the one hundred fiftieth anniversary of Lincoln's birth and was placed at the summit of Route 30, the old Lincoln Highway, in 1959. In 1968 it was moved to its present location.

The statue stands twelve and a half feet high atop a thirty-foot marble base. It was financed by the late Dr. Charles W. Jeffrey, a Rawlins philanthropist. The town of Jeffrey City, originally called Home-on-the-Range, was named for the generous doctor. Near the statue a Wyoming State Travel Information office is open during the summer.

As you drive the last fifteen miles into Laramie, think what it must have been like to travel the route on horseback. President Theodore Roosevelt and U. S. Senator Francis E. Warren set out on horseback from Laramie to Warren's ranch near Cheyenne on May 30, 1903. President Roosevelt rode the entire fifty-six miles, but Warren got tired and dropped out.

✒

*Answer: Vedauwoo is an Arapaho word meaning "earth-born."

About the Close-Up

•• What is it like, running the only gasoline station and store within forty-nine miles, eight thousand feet above sea level? Betty and Bob Reeder share some stories about Lonetree Junction and the people who have stopped here.

Close-Up: BETTY & BOB REEDER

MOST TRAVELERS DRIVE right by the gasoline station and convenience store at Lonetree Junction, halfway between Cheyenne and Laramie. But people who stop are grateful they are there. This is the only gasoline station on the forty-nine mile stretch between the two cities, and it has the only public telephone.

The owner sells sandwiches, convenience foods, groceries, and beer, and also runs a post office. A pool table and a massive wooden bar carved with brands from nearby ranches fill an adjoining room. But the reason most people stop at this outpost eight thousand feet above sea level is to buy gasoline.

"I-80 doesn't come through downtown Cheyenne," Betty Reeder said. "Everybody thinks there'll be a place to turn off

This statue of Abraham Lincoln by Robert Russin is on the summit between Cheyenne and Laramie. (Wyoming State Museum)

later, and the next thing they know, they're on the Interstate heading for Laramie. People don't realize gas stations aren't on every corner like they are in the cities. In Wyoming they're few and far between." Reeder and her son Bob owned the station until December 1992.

Gasoline costs more at Lonetree than it does in Laramie or Cheyenne. That's because the owner has to pay more for it.

The gasoline station and store stay open from 7 A.M to at least 10 P.M. seven days a week. The owner also runs a twenty-four hour towing service.

Betty and her husband bought the station as a retirement business in 1980 and moved here from New Jersey with their son Bob and his family. At first, the Reeders lived behind the station, but after Betty's husband died, both Betty and Bob and his household moved to Cheyenne. The mother and son then commuted together.

"It's a nice drive," Betty said in 1991. "There isn't much traffic on the road, and you see all the wildlife—coyotes, antelope—the other morning we saw seven big bull elks."

"We like it out here, the open spaces and clean air. The cleanest air in America is right here," said Bob.

"You meet all kinds of people here," said Betty, "And they do things you would never believe. People really don't use their heads sometimes, especially in the winter. People who live around here!

"One winter two men and two women from Laramie had been to a dance in Cheyenne. The women had on high-heeled shoes, silk stockings, no boots, and the snow was four feet deep. Their car broke down in the underpass. Those women were frostbitten. We built a fire and got some blankets, and they called someone in Laramie to take them home."

"Last winter some people were four-wheel driving in Vedauwoo," Bob said. "The road was closed, but they went back in there anyway and got stuck. The lady was pregnant, and she went into labor, and I had to go back in there and rescue her. I didn't bother with the car—I just wanted to get her out of there." The couple used the Reeders' phone to call for a ride to the hospital.

Betty's training as a registered nurse came in handy sometimes. "One time a man came in, and he looked terrible. I said, 'Don't you feel well?'

"He said 'No.'

"I said 'What's wrong?'

"He said he had just gotten out of a hospital back East. He'd had a heart attack and was driving to Centennial all by himself to stay with some friends.

"I drove his car and I took him fifty-five miles to Centennial. My son followed me in his car. He was lucky this place was here; otherwise I don't know where he would have gone."

Betty and Bob Reeder enjoyed meeting all kinds of people at Lone Tree Junction and tell stories of unusual customers.

They heard a lot of hard luck stories, Betty said—lost wallets, money used up on car repairs with nothing left for gasoline or food. "Sometimes you believe them and sometimes you don't. I'll usually give them enough gasoline to get to town, but I can't afford to fill up gas tanks. I'll feed the kids. I'll feed older people too, but they should know better."

A lot of people tried to trade goods for gasoline, Bob said—tools, furniture, even a waterbed. "We'd see people eating out of trash cans. They get off the trains and wander around. One old man used to just walk the barrow pits. We'd give them a sandwich and a soda. I'd feel kind of sorry for them."

"A few years ago we had a storm so bad, everybody was afraid to drive," said Betty. "We had about twenty people here. They slept on the floor, on the pool table, on the bar...."

Occasionally their telephone went out. "It's underground cable, and I guess animals chew on it," said Betty. "Lightning puts it out a lot. They have to come from Pine Bluffs to fix it."

Although the Reeders had some problems with petty theft, only once did anyone threaten violence, and that was when Betty and her husband lived behind the station.

"A man came one time—he was banging on the windows and doors at 5:30 in the morning. He wanted gas. I always got up with my husband when anybody came in like that.

"My husband told him the gas would be ten dollars extra because we weren't open, and he said he didn't care. But when my husband went to ring up the sale on the man's credit card and explained to him about the ten dollars again, the guy grabbed my husband and pinned down his arms.

"I had a gun in my pocket—we always had a gun with us. I told him to let my husband go.

"He said, 'What for?'

"I took out the gun and pointed it at him. I said, 'You let him go or I'm going to shoot.' He knew I meant it, too.

"He left then, but he broke our big plate glass window. We called the sheriff, and they caught up with him at Vedauwoo and booked him in the Laramie jail. He had to pay for everything. He'd left his credit card, so we knew who he was."

✧

Don Sammons bought the Reeders' business in December 1992 and is expanding it, according to Buford resident and part-time station employee Naomi Heitzman. Sammons sells some groceries and is planning to add motel rooms and hookups for RVs. In April 1993 Heitzman said the interstate was "solid ice" and the station was filled with stranded truckers.

Chapter 5

Laramie

LARAMIE, Wyoming's third largest city
Population: 26,687   *Elevation*: 7,165
* Question: Where is Laramie's "tree area"?

Places to Visit

•• Visitors' Center in caboose on Third Street, south side of town.

•• Wyoming Territorial Park, 975 Snowy Range Road. See Close-up.

•• Laramie Plains Museum in 1892 mansion, 603 Ivinson Avenue. Guided Tour. Small fee.

•• Children's Museum and Nature Center, 710 Garfield Street (Laramie Plains Civic Center). Call (307) 745-6332 for hours and fees.

•• Day-long railroad excursion through Snowy Range and to a guest ranch near Walden, Colorado. Mid-May through December. Call (307) 742-9162 for schedule and prices.

•• Albany County Cattlewomen summer barbecues on nearby ranches. Alternate Thursday nights. Check local paper for schedule and more information.

•• Free summer Wednesday night band concerts in Washington Park (also a good place to picnic). Park is bordered by Sheridan, Rainbow, Eighteenth and Twenty-First streets.

•• University of Wyoming, free admission
  • Geology museum, northwest part of quad (Prexy's Pasture). Look for life-size Tyrannosaurus Rex out front. See Close-up.
  • Planetarium, Bioscience Building basement, near Ninth Street. Weekly shows when University is in session. Call (307) 766-6150.
  • Anthropology Museum, Anthropology Building, Ivinson Avenue at Fourteenth Street.
  • Art Museum, lower level of Fine Arts Center, east of Fraternity Row.
  • Gallery 234 (art) in University Union, east end of Prexy's Pasture near Thirteenth Street. Union also has bookstore, cafeteria, and late afternoon-evening pub.
  • Chamber music festival. Concerts in June.
  • Jelm Mountain Infrared Observatory, south of Laramie. Take Highway 230 to Woods Landing and go south on County Road 10. Call (307) 766-6150 for information.
  • American Heritage Center (archives), top floor, Coe Library, Thirteenth and Ivinson Avenue. See Close-up.
  • The University has many special events and lecture series. Check at information desk in University Union.
•• University of Wyoming, admission charged
  •Summer repertory theatre, alternate weekends.
  •Summer international dinners with entertainment.

A Brief Background

Laramie is home of the only four-year college or university in the state, founded in 1886. Because the University draws students and faculty from foreign countries, Laramie has a more diverse population than most Wyoming towns.

You can see the sports arena, nicknamed "Dome on the Range," from nearly anywhere in town. University football and basketball games bring fans from throughout the state.

For visitors to the main campus, the University provides free parking on Fourteenth Street between Grand Avenue and Garfield Street. The library and University Union are near Thirteenth Street and Ivinson Avenue.

The oldest campus buildings are of native sandstone. The University had its own quarry. The quad is called Prexy's Pasture, and the white marble sculpture in the middle is Robert Russin's *The Family*, unveiled in 1983. Russin, who was the University's artist-in-residence, said *The Family* represents people caring for people and can be interpreted as professors with their students or students who bring their families to the University.

One of the most loyal of all UW alumni is Ralph McWhinnie, who enrolled as a freshman in 1917 and has been associated with the University ever since. McWhinnie Hall, in the northeast corner of Prexy's Pasture, was named for him.

McWhinnie was University Registrar until 1968. Since then he has been unofficial UW historian. His office in Knight Hall contains handwritten academic senate minutes from the 1920s and minutes of the 1931 meeting when students decided to strike, in protest to then-President Crane's tactless reaction to four young people found "necking" in a car during intermission at a University dance. The strike was short-lived because the University took away striking students' work-study grants, and that spelled disaster during the Depression.

The University runs a pilot elementary school on campus and provides an extensive outreach program: from agricultural extension agents, to classes taught by telecommunication, to "flying professors" who teach weekly classes throughout the state.

Southwest of town at Jelm Mountain stands the Wyoming Infrared Observatory, which has the most powerful infrared telescope in the continental United States, second only to one which NASA built in Hawaii. The ninety-two-inch telescope is so sensitive, it can detect new stars hidden behind clouds of cosmic dust fifteen hundred light years away. The facility has the most sophisticated telescope control system in the world.

The six-mile trip from the town of Jelm to the observatory is a thrill in itself. One hairpin turn follows another on the road described by one University of Wyoming astronomer as "one lane or less." The observatory stands 9,656 feet above sea level. University of Wyoming astronomers need not only Ph.D.s, but also expertise in driving and plowing. In winter they drive to their three-day shifts in SnoCats.

Laramie has long, cold winters. Temperatures usually fall to minus thirty degrees for at least a few days each year. Visiting sports teams carry oxygen and pray they won't get snowed in after the game. Winter outdoor sports flourish, especially skiing in the Snowy Range.

The snowiest months are March, April, and May. Laramie has a short growing season, and to grow a tomato outdoors is a major accomplishment. When John Wideman taught at UW, he wrote, in his novel *Damballah*, that spring in Laramie should have its own name—like "shit" or "disaster."

North of Laramie, Albany County has several one-room ranch schools, where teachers live on the ranch and may be snowed in most of the winter. Some schools have only one pupil. To attend high school, students must board in Laramie or Wheatland.

Native Americans roamed the Laramie plains ten thousand years go, but the city's name honors the first known Euro-American in the area, Jacques La Ramie, a fur trapper who disappeared in 1820 and may have been killed by Arapahos.

The present-day city started in 1866 as a tent and shanty town along what is now Spring Creek Road. The shanty town moved closer to the proposed railroad tracks when General Grenville Dodge completed the Union Pacific survey the following year. Like Cheyenne, early Laramie was "hell-on-wheels." Its first mayor, Melville C. Brown, resigned after three weeks in office because he couldn't keep Laramie's unruly citizens under control.

Laramie's most famous nineteenth century resident was journalist and humorist Bill Nye. Nye came from Wisconsin in 1875 to "find himself." (In 1990 Wyoming's Centennial slogan was "Find yourself in Wyoming.") Nye stayed seven years, then returned east and spent several years on the lecture circuit with poet James Whitcomb Riley. In Laramie he is remembered for naming and publishing the Laramie *Boomerang*, a daily newspaper still in circulation. To supplement his income he also practiced law and served as Laramie's postmaster and justice of the peace.

Nye named the paper after a stray mule who had adopted him on a Laramie street. Years later, miffed because the corporation which owned the *Boomerang* owed him money (which it never repaid), Nye commented that the name suited the paper, because it was "a missile that frequently returns and smites him who had launched it."

Nye was twenty-five when he arrived in Laramie, and he had thirty-five cents to his name. In one of his rare serious *Boomerang* columns, he answered a young man who asked whether it would be wise for him to go West:

> The advantage of the West for the young man consists in this: that he is there given a chance to show his gait and demonstrate his merits. He is as good a man with a $5 suit of clothes and a bobtail genealogy as any other man if he be a good citizen and pan out all right. Nobody asks him who his grandfather was, and

why he came West.... I could be poor and come near-
er to enjoying it in the West than anywhere else.

⤳

***Answer: Laramie's "tree area" runs for about a mile and
a half starting just south of the University campus. Most
homes here were built in the fifties, and the original owners planted the trees, mainly fruitless mulberry.**

About the Close-Ups

•• Thinking of spending a day at the Territorial Park? Let
Maureen Murphy, one of the park's founders, tell you what
you can expect.

•• Brent Breithaupt is curator of one of Wyoming's most popular museums. He can also tell you about dinosaur fossils
throughout the state.

•• You'd never guess what's stored in the University archives.
Would you believe, Jack Benny's violin? Hopalong Cassidy's
revolver? Amelia Earhart's aviation records? Meet the hitchhiking historian who acquired these: Gene Gressley.

•• Lucile Russell has been "visiting" Laramie ever since she
was 29, and she has been an asset to the town ever since.

•• Tom Armajo grew up on the Wind River Reservation north
of Interstate 80, and has ideas about how the reservation
should change.

•• In Wyoming people tend to judge individuals for who they
are rather than by ethnic background, says Delores Cardona,
Director of Minority Affairs at the University. This individu-
alism can be both a benefit and a disadvantage to people of
minority backgrounds.

Close-Up: WYOMING TERRITORIAL PARK

SOME SAY THE WYOMING Territorial Park originated in Maureen Murphy's kitchen, in 1983.

Laramie's Territorial Prison was falling into ruin, and Murphy and some other Laramie citizens wanted it restored. Some Chamber of Commerce members formed a committee and met at Murphy's home. That committee evolved into the Wyoming Territorial Prison Corporation, a non-profit agency which oversees the park today.

"Our mission is to tell the history of Wyoming and the West, from settlement to statehood," said Murphy. "We want it to be educational and historical—but we also want it to be fun."

The cornerstone of the park is the prison, which was to hold "Evil Doers of All Kinds" when it opened in 1872. It is one of only four territorial prisons ever built and one of two still standing today. The U. S. Marshal's Service ran it until 1890. Wyoming was granted statehood that year and the prison became a state facility. The Territorial Prison closed after the state penitentiary at Rawlins opened in 1902.

The University of Wyoming used the grounds then as an experimental stock farm, but abandoned the main building in 1978 because it needed repairs.

Albany County citizens, who had earlier turned down a tax increase for recreational facilities, passed a one-cent sales tax boost in 1986 to restore the prison. In 1989 they passed another sales tax increase to develop the one hundred eighty acres surrounding the prison. The project was named the Wyoming Territorial Park and the site donated to the State of Wyoming.

"We realized that only to save the prison wouldn't work," Murphy said. "We needed other attractions too."

The park corporation called in as consultant Dr. Robert Birney, retired vice-president of development at Colonial Williamsburg, Virginia, who visited the Laramie site three times.

Ultimately the Territorial Park will cost sixty-five million dollars, and its founders hope it will become the Rocky

Mountain region's largest Western heritage attraction. Completed to date are the restored prison; an "End-of Tracks" frontier railroad town with a general store, saloon, doctor/dentist/barber office, and blacksmith shop; the old horse barn, with a restaurant and dinner theatre upstairs and craftspeople demonstrating frontier folk art on the ground floor; a livery stable where visitors can rent horses for trail rides or children can buy pony rides; an operating stagecoach; an amphitheater; and an outdoor barbecue restaurant.

Still to come are a railroad depot, Indian camp, military post, and natural history center.

The park is open every day from nine A.M. to eight P.M. from Memorial Weekend through Labor Day, then weekends through mid-October. Hour-long prison tours are offered daily, year-round.

"We agreed we were not going to glorify criminals," Murphy said. "For every criminal we spotlight, we also spotlight a lawman."

The U. S. Marshal's Exhibit, from the Smithsonian Institution, is a major attraction. So is the women's gallery, featuring the first woman justice of the peace, first woman governor, first female bailiff, and first woman to vote in a general election—all Wyomingites.

People can take the prison tour more than once without losing interest, since tours vary according to the guides, who research their special interests. Apart from the tours, visitors can watch three-minute dramatic portrayals on video of prisoners and lawmen from the past.

The most famous person incarcerated here was George Leroy Parker, alias Butch Cassidy from Utah, who signed in, in 1894, as George Cassidy from New York. He explained later that he lied about his identity to protect the reputations of his thirteen brothers and sisters. They all led law-abiding lives

The Wyoming Territorial Prison is the focal point of the historic park which has been built around it. (Wyoming Territorial Park)

except for one brother, who robbed a stagecoach. Parker was in prison for stealing horses.

Parker made many friends in prison, and the governor pardoned him in 1896, after Parker promised "never to molest the State of Wyoming again." He broke his promise three years later, when he held up a train near Rock River.

Security at the territorial prison was lax at first. One-fourth of the inmates escaped during the first two years the prison was open. One strolled off the grounds to freedom after feeding his pet deer. A soft-hearted warden used to bring young inmates home to his ranch to provide them a wholesome environment. He was eventually fired.

The park corporation takes pride in the historical accuracy of the restored prison and the End-of-Track buildings in the park. In contrast, scriptwriters for the free shows given every

Butch Cassidy, an alias of George LeRoy Parker, served time at the Wyoming Territorial Prison. (Wyoming Territorial Park)

hour in the amphitheater and the Bird of Paradise Saloon make no attempt to portray reality. They go for laughs, drawing from frontier stereotypes.

Most Laramie residents have enthusiastically supported the Territorial Park since it opened in 1991. "This project has really given the community a rallying point," Murphy said. "Laramie was always the home of the University, but it seemed as though the University wasn't ours—it belonged to the state. This park is something we can claim for ourselves. I'm pleased and amazed with the number of people who buy season passes and keep coming back."

Another plus is that the park provides summer employment for local residents and University of Wyoming students.

A dinner theatre upstairs in the Horse Barn, open every night except Monday, sold out its first season's performances. Murphy described the entertainment as a blend of vaudeville, melodrama, and patriotism. The theme is Old West, and most performers are University of Wyoming students, who call on the audience to participate. Dinner is all-you-can-eat barbecue served family style.

For information on schedules and prices, call this toll-free number: 1-800-845-2287.

Close-Up: UW GEOLOGY MUSEUM

A SKELETON OF THE HUGE plant-eating dinosaur Apatosaurus (Brontosaurus) stretches the length of the museum's first floor. A skull of a mammoth, killed by prehistoric hunters, represents a time when Wyoming's climate was even colder than it is today.

Remains of ferns, coral, a palm tree, squid, crocodile, a huge turtle, and a giant stingray mark an era when the land here was below sea level and the climate tropical.

"We can look at these things and imagine what the area was like at the time," said Brent Breithaupt, curator of the University of Wyoming Geology Museum.

Most of the museum collections originated in Wyoming, and they have universal appeal. Fossils of a rhinoceros, a camel, and a giant pig attract people of all ages. An exhibit on the balcony displays dinosaur nests and eggs and invites visitors to discover what dinosaur skin felt like. Another shows the evolution of the horse over fifty million years. From the ceiling hangs a reproduction of a flying reptile.

The museum has rock and mineral displays, including one on the volcanic origin of diamonds, which are found in

Wyoming south of Laramie. But fossils capture the attention of most museum visitors—especially dinosaur fossils.

"Almost anywhere you go in Wyoming there's someone doing some paleontology work," Breithaupt said. "We have people from Yale, Michigan, the National Museum of History in New York, Chicago.... This is just a very rich region of the world for fossils."

Most discoveries are made on federal or private land, Breithaupt said. Wyoming has no claim on these, although University of Colorado paleontologist Robert Bakker, who supervised the most recent diggings at Como Bluff northwest of Laramie, has promised to display reconstructions of those findings in a museum at Rock River, Wyoming.

Breithaupt called Como Bluff one of the richest dinosaur sites ever discovered. "There are lots of fossils to be found," Breithaupt said. "There are a lot of miles in Wyoming—a lot of miles that have never been walked—and a lot of people who have walked over fossils and not recognized them.

"There's so much here to begin with, and nature is exposing these fossils to the surface on a regular basis. New things weather out every year. There are other places with dinosaur fossils, but they're hundreds of thousands of feet beneath the earth. Here rocks are close to the surface—they are uplifted."

The best way to visit dinosaur sites in Wyoming is to join a group tour, Breithaupt said. "Como Bluff is mostly on private land. It's just not a place where you can go and poke around on your own." Breithaupt leads a day tour to Como Bluff during the summer.

"It's gotten to the point that we have three hundred people showing up. We may have to require advance registration and hold more than one tour on consecutive weekends."

The museum displays only a small percentage of its collections, Breithaupt said. Most are kept in back rooms, for

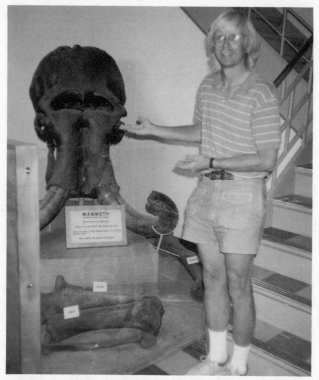

Brent Breithaupt is the curator of the UW Geology Museum, which houses a rich collection of dinosaur fossils.

teaching and research, or are lent to researchers in other universities. Breithaupt changes the museum exhibits often.

The trend now is for museums to display cast reproductions rather than original skeletons, Breithaupt said. "They're lighter, less fragile, and we have less to worry about. It's the best way to protect the specimen." Specimens not on display are also easier to teach with. The light-colored bones on the Apatosaurus skeleton are reproductions.

Media coverage of fossil controversies has created a renewed interest in the UW Geology Museum. Dinosaur fossils discovered in northern Wyoming recently were taken to the Museum of the Rockies in Montana. These were discovered on federal lands, Breithaupt said, and could have gone anywhere within the United States.

"We have a wonderful cooperation with the Museum of the Rockies," Breithaupt said. The museum may send UW a reconstruction of one of the specimens. Breithaupt said the department is expanding and the museum continually adds new exhibits, but at this point isn't equipped to house any new major findings.

Museums in even the smallest Wyoming towns include exhibits of fossils, rocks, and minerals. Displays can be found at Fossil Butte National Monument near Kemmerer, Western Wyoming College in Rock Springs, Tait Museum at Casper, and at the museum at Rock River. But the University Museum is core.

"This is the main paleontology facility in Wyoming," Breithaupt said. "This would be the main place to go."

Close-up: GENE GRESSLEY

GENE GRESSLEY WAS TWENTY-FIVE when he started his career as archivist at the University of Wyoming. He came with a graduate degree in history—and ambition. The university archives held 284 collections then. Today, thanks to Gressley, the archives hold more than thirteen thousand collections of personal and professional papers and artifacts, in three Laramie locations.

These are some of the items you can find there: a first edition of *The Book of Mormon*; a first edition of *The Wizard of Oz;* a test record by Bing Crosby marked, "This guy won't make it"; the private papers of the U. S. Navy commander at Pearl Harbor on December 7, 1941; the complete files of the Wyoming Stock Growers Association; musical arrangements by Harry James; Barbara Stanwyck's Oscar; Owen Wister's desk.

Archives figured low in the University's budget in 1956, when Gressley arrived in Laramie. He knew he couldn't acquire new material without getting out and talking with people, but his transportation allowance was just four hundred dollars a year. So Gressley hit the road anyway—he hitchhiked.

"I used to take two suitcases, a forty-pound tape recorder, and one of these accordion briefcases. When you're on the road for six weeks, you bring a lot of stuff. And once you got on the road you stayed, because it was actually cheap to stay out there."

The university paid nine dollars a day for in-state travel and eleven dollars a day out-of-state. "I used to pay seven dollars for a hotel room. That left me four dollars for food. I stayed at a bawdy house in New York once, although I didn't realize it until later. I just thought the girls in the lobby were friendly."

Thanks to Dr. William Fitzhugh Jr., son of a Wyoming oil magnate, Gressley's hitchhiking lasted just four years. Gressley wrote to Fitzhugh in 1960 requesting his father's papers. Dr. Fitzhugh complied, then called Gressley and asked, "Do you collect rare books?"

"I told him, 'We'd love to, but we don't have any budget.' He said he would help."

Gressley traveled to California to visit Fitzhugh, hitchhiking part of the way and going the rest of the way by bus. He rented a room at the Manx Hotel in San Francisco. Fitzhugh came to see him.

"Dr. Fitzhugh charged into the lobby of the Manx Hotel and boomed out, 'Gressley! Why are you staying in a fleabag place like this?'

"I was really shy then, really easily embarrassed. I told him this was what my budget allowed. He turned on his heels, walked up the street to the St. Francis, got a bellhop, brought him back, and moved me into the St. Francis Hotel. When we got to my room he said, 'I'm going to call your President.' He got on the phone then and called [former University

In the late 1950s Gene Gressley hitchhiked across the U.S. to build UW's collection of archival papers and artifacts.

of Wyoming President] Duke Humphrey and chewed him out for sending his people out without any support.

"From then on, I had no trouble getting travel money. This is, to me, such a minimal investment for what you get. Archives is the public relations arm of the university. When we tell people, 'We want your papers,' they realize, 'They're interested in me, not just my money.'

"I wasn't looking for money, I was looking for papers. But so many people we dealt with were very wealthy, the archives turned out to be one of our best money raisers."

Dr. William Fitzhugh sent the University of Wyoming fifty thousand dollars a year for the next ten years, Gressley said. A room in the archives is named for him.

Gressley takes pride in the Anaconda Collection: twelve hundred file drawers of economic geological reports and more than fifty file drawers of geological maps. "You never do anything in this world by yourself. All I did in acquiring the Anaconda collection—I discovered the collection, I found out who to deal with, and I served as a clearinghouse for the lobby." The late Governor Ed Herschler brought a delegation to Denver in his private plane to lobby Anaconda, Gressley said.

The University of Wyoming archives has the journals and letters of one hundred sixty western writers—more than any other university archives.

"I've taken more criticism for our Hollywood collection than anything else. People think if it's Hollywood, it must be ephemeral. We have Barbara Stanwyck's papers, David Niven's, Eleanor Powell's, Jane Powell's, Jack Benny's, many producers and directors.... We have the largest collection of film music and screen writers anywhere, and a wonderful collection of big band leaders.

"When I'd go to Hollywood I used to see eighty to one hundred people a week. I'd have them to dinner—you can see a lot of people that way—or I'd have breakfasts or lunches. We didn't get to talk at big occasions like that, but they didn't care. They basically just wanted to see this character from Wyoming who was running all around the place."

On his return trip he'd meet with people individually. "You see one person, one time, you're not going to get a collection. You're asking for something for nothing. You have to be willing to listen; you have to establish credibility; you have to answer letters and follow through. I used to write twenty thousand letters a year—ten thousand form letters and ten thousand individual ones. I worked seven days a week—I still do."

Acquiring Jack Benny's papers tested Gressley's perseverance. Gressley met Benny through Lucille Ball's head scriptwriter, who invited Gressley to watch an *I Love Lucy* rehearsal. Jack Benny was guest star. Gressley asked the writer where Benny's papers were. The writer asked Benny. "He said, 'Hmm! They're in my basement.'

"Two-thirds of the way through the rehearsal Benny passed Milt [the writer] a note that said, 'Bring your friend over to my house after the rehearsal.'

"That was one of the more difficult evenings I've spent. Jack Benny was very gracious but very reserved. I had to talk and talk and talk.

"That evening was repeated several times, over dinner. Jack Benny was one of the more shy, difficult people I met. He never said what he would do. When he died, he left his papers to his wife and daughter. So I went to see Mary Livingston. She was just the opposite of Jack, a regular chatterbox."

Mary Livingston didn't give Gressley Benny's papers either. "A few years later their daughter, Joan, called. She said they were selling the big house, and that everybody was after her father's papers, but in all fairness they should go to us because we'd been asking for them for so long."

Personal collections can contain "everything," Gressley said—"pieces of clothing, check stubs, grocery receipts, all sorts of things." At the top of Jack Benny's papers was a receipt from a poultry company for sixteen chickens.

"Barbara Stanwyck sent us all her scripts, with the stills [photos] bound in with the scripts. She'd signed them all for us. She was a very gracious lady.

"I found people incredibly helpful. I was never a threat to them so they looked at me differently from people in the industry. I was philanthropy, so I saw their best side.

"People used to say, 'You know, Gene, I should probably give this to UCLA [University of California at Los Angeles],' and I'd say, 'That's fine. Did they ask you for it?' People are not going to bring in their papers anywhere without someone asking for them.

"What I collected was heavily twentieth-century material. I would love to get ranch records from the 1880s; I'd love to collect nineteenth-century mining records. But you can't find them today. We're leaving something for the twenty-first century. Fifty to one hundred years from now this archives will be valued much more than it is today."

A visit to the University of Wyoming archives is a must for anyone doing serious research on mining history, petroleum history, livestock, conservation, water, economic geology, aviation, mountaineering, journalism, western literary writers, big bands, screen writers, or film music, Gressley said.

"But we won't keep that cutting edge if we don't keep acquiring material. We'll become a mausoleum, not an archives."

Today the University's emphasis is on maintaining the collections it has rather than acquiring new ones. Some papers and artifacts are on the third floor of the University's Coe Library. The rest are stored in two Laramie warehouses. A new American Heritage Center on campus will hold at least one warehouseful, Gressley said. Even so, anyone wishing to see specific collections should make an appointment, so librarians can have these on hand.

Gressley left the University of Wyoming in 1993. He said his father, a Congregational minister, was his role model. "My father always said, 'Ask for anything you want in this life; be polite, and be persistent.'"

Close-Up: LUCILE O. RUSSELL

LUCILE RUSSELL CAME TO Laramie from Houston to visit her uncle when she was twenty-nine. "I've been visiting him ever since," she said. "He's even died, and I'm still here.

"Laramie is a place that grows on you. You hate it when you first come here, then find yourself staying and liking it. I like the size of the town. I like the opportunities. Opportunities present themselves here to those who help themselves."

For twelve years Russell was director of the Laramie Neighborhood Center. "That was in Optimist Park, on the west side of town. We worked with low-income families, and I had a nice staff of four people. It was under the Snowy Range Community Action Agency," Russell said.

The center offered tutoring for children, literacy classes for adults and recreational activities. So successful was the program under Russell's direction that in 1979, Russell received special recognition for distinguished community service from the *Laramie Daily Boomerang* and the Laramie Lions Club. A plaque in the Albany County Courthouse bears her name. The community service award is given annually and is celebrated at a banquet which Russell attends each year.

The Neighborhood Center relied partly on donations from local merchants. Russell said that when she was assistant director, the agency director asked his fraternity brother, who owned a hardware store, to lend him a stapler. The owner turned him down. Then Russell approached the same merchant. He lent her the stapler and gave her all the staples she would need.

"He knew me. We belonged to the same church, and he knew I was trustworthy. Just because you're in the same fraternity doesn't mean you know that person. I brought the stapler and staples back to the director and said, 'Don't send a baby to do a man's job. Here they are.'

"That never set well with him, and afterwards I was sorry I'd said that. Now I always tell myself, 'Put yourself in the other fellow's shoes when he's down. Don't kick him when he's down, kick him when he's up!'

Lucile Russell came to Laramie to visit her uncle when she was twenty-nine. She's been serving the community ever since.

"There weren't many people here I'd ask for things that wouldn't give me what I asked for. A lot of people knew my husband before they knew me. He worked as janitor for a bank in town. If I presented myself as Mrs. James Russell, that opened the door for me. But I didn't want to live on his coattails. I wanted to do it on my own."

Years ago Russell helped found Modern Matrons, a social club for African-American women in Laramie. "We bought benches for the park. We built our own clubhouse from the ground, at 765 North Pine. It was bought and paid for by us." Eventually the club disbanded, and the clubhouse was put up for sale.

Russell works part-time at the Albany County Library, has been president several times of Church Women United, and volunteers at Interfaith Clearing House, a United Way agency. "Most of the time, if I think it's a good cause, I will volunteer and help."

Her two children are grown and live in Seattle. "Laramie is a nice place to rear kids," Russell said. "I think my children were happy here. They knew they had to make life what they wanted it to be for themselves, not what other people wanted."

But Laramie doesn't have a very large black community. "If there's a black church, there's more whites attending it than there are blacks."

Even so, Russell said, if she had her life to live over, she would still choose Laramie as her home. "I just want to be labeled as a human being. There's no reason we can't be, if we carry ourselves in the manner we should carry ourselves. My kids tell me that's impossible. They say, 'They're always going to have that stigma on you.'

"I'm out of the limelight now, and I want to stay out of it," said Russell. "Sometimes I think I'm getting tired, because I think some of the people who come into the Clearing House for help could help themselves. "Sometimes I just want to go home, play my bridge and play my pinochle and forget it."

Close Up: TOM ARMAJO

TOM ARMAJO LIVES AND works in Laramie, but his thoughts turn often to the Wind River Reservation, where he was born and raised.

His father, an Arapaho, and his mother, a Shoshone, were alcoholics, and his father committed suicide when Tom was eleven. "I stayed with my grandmother as long as I could. My mother would come and get me whenever she needed money.

Once the money was spent, she'd release the kids. I rolled winos to get money then."

The money his mother spent came from the "per capita," an allotment given to each member of the tribe as a share in mineral royalties. The reservation is rich in oil, and during the seventies, the per capita could be as high as a thousand dollars a month. It is perhaps one-tenth of that now.

From the age of eleven on, Armajo lived with twenty-seven sets of foster parents. He has ten brothers and sisters and four half-brothers and sisters, but he doesn't know them well. Two institutions helped him. The Church of Latter Day Saints accepted him into a special program in the State of Washington, where he finished high school.

"As soon as I got out of high school I had to find a home. The military became my home. It was the best thing that ever happened to me. They taught me to believe in myself, to set goals." He was a member of the U.S. Airborne Rangers for three years.

Armajo became the first Arapaho to serve on a Mormon mission, spending a year in London, England. He taught classes in mountaineering, scuba diving, sky diving and survival techniques at Brigham Young University, where he met his wife, a Navajo. Recently he completed a degree in accounting at the University of Wyoming.

"We've lived in Arizona, Utah, and Wyoming," he said. "Of all the places we've been, Laramie is the most comfortable. This is a place for my family to grow. They accept races here. Sometimes they have conflicts, usually connected with alcohol, but I don't have that much problem myself, maybe because I'm so outspoken."

Armajo said he doesn't fit in on the reservation. He estimates the unemployment rate on the reservation as between sixty-three and eighty-three per cent. "They have a few high-salaried people and some very low-salaried people. The biggest paying jobs are at the Bureau of Indian Affairs, the schools, and small businesses." He said the large chain stores in the area hire no Native Americans.

"You have to remember, a lot of Anglo people don't get hired on the reservation because of Indian preference. We do have this race segregation. There are businesses [in Lander and Riverton] where their major customers are people from the reservation—but they don't hire Indians.

"What I'd like to see is more economic development on the reservation. When Indians start owning their own businesses and start competing, it may get better."

The Arapaho tribe operates a cultural center and a summer language program for children, but Armajo wants it to do more.

"We rely so heavily on the federal government to come through on our projects. If we had our own foundations, we could take care of our orphanages; we could take care of our alcohol programs.

"Right now we have so much management turnover. People use our resources as a stepping stone. Usually federal monies come into play for three years. The grant runs out, and the manager doesn't know how to apply for a new grant, so he moves on. After about two years we get the programs back."

Alcohol rehabilitation should include employment programs, Armajo said. "If you show them there's a better way of life and throw them back in the same old pot, there's no change. There's just no jobs. People are stuck in a cycle that they're unable to break by themselves.

"This reservation is one of a kind, partly because of the access of roads, partly because of the wealth. It's created a different kind of people from any other Indian I've seen. It's created more strife between families. The only ones who have benefited from the wealth are the half-breeds. The half-

Tom Armajo, an Arapaho who was raised on Wind River Reservation, has ideas about how the reservation should change.

breeds control the reservation. The full-bloods don't plan ahead—everything's here and now. They have something, they give it away.

"If you've been to South America, Mexico, or another culture and seen how they live, then come to the reservation and see what goes on there—there's no difference in people. The people are basically the same. But there's more community action, more development in other places. It's something the Indians have to do for themselves, it's got to be internal. They have to have a goal and an objective.

"We were once a very large tribe, but we were massacred. We were like the buffalo—killed off. The way I see the old men of the past, they believed in commitment. They believed in something so strong, they were willing to die for it. I don't see that in our leaders now.

"I can't change what exists on the reservation, but I'm trying. I have two uncles on the tribal council, and I feel they're doing a good job. When my cousin Chester Armajo was alive, a lot did change. We were able to start a store and get our money that had been in escrow. [Former Secretary of the Interior] James Watt helped us a lot—and Ronald Reagan. Watt tried to get the tribes into the oil industry, but our tribe wasn't ready for it. In the future they may be."

The tribe recently set up a one-million-dollar foundation, including matching state funds, to send its young people to the University of Wyoming. Seven students are enrolled under that program, Armajo said. "When they graduate and pay back, we'll be able to send more." In 1991, fewer than 100 Arapahos, Shoshones, and members of other Indian nations were enrolled at the University of Wyoming.

The scholarship program has some problems, and in 1991 the tribe demanded an audit of the fund held by the University. "The University's not fair to some of the kids," Armajo said. Some come off the reservation and they're not ready for the University, but the University doesn't tell them that. They are not getting the nurturing care they need.

"We should have bought a house in Laramie, as a base for the future. Then we could have our own people employed in the program. I told the council, but it fell on deaf ears."

Ideally, Armajo sees the Wind River Reservation as independent of the Bureau of Indian Affairs, as a separate county in Wyoming. But he knows that isn't likely to be. He does have other hopes for the future.

"I see taxation changing, where the land on the reservation is taxed as a source of income to our tribe. I see more economic trade, an international airport, and foreign investors dealing directly with the reservation. I'd like to see the per capita used for education instead of paid individually. I'd like to see labor unions on the reservations and co-op stores.

"I see the reservation as a good place to live, a safe place to live. Reservations are beautiful places to be if you don't associate with a lot of the people. It's the place where I grew up; it's home. But I don't want my kids to have any part of it the way it is now.

"I think where our heart is is where home is. Years ago my grandmother told me I would help my people a lot. Sometimes we do things we believe in—it may take twenty, thirty years for people to believe us, trust us.

"When the majority of the people want a big enough change, it will happen. Once they are able to change their lives, they can touch each other's lives. But we have a long ways to go."

Close-Up: DOLORES CARDONA

"WYOMING IS A VERY individualistic state," said Dolores Cardona, Director of Minority Affairs at the University of Wyoming.

"There's racism here—there's racism everywhere you go. But if you do stand your ground and contribute and get involved with people, people here tend to be a little more responsive than in other places—people tend to accept you as an individual.

"That's the positive side of this individualized streak that Wyoming people have. There's a negative in that it's hard to organize and do some collective things. The minority community is very much 'families helping families,' kind of a group thing."

Cardona and her staff offer support services to Asian American, African American, Hispanic, and Native American students. She said some students she works with object to the term "Minority."

"Some of them grew up in Wyoming in the only non-Anglo family in town. They are used to being treated as individuals."

Hispanics are the largest non-Anglo presence in Wyoming, followed by Native Americans. But while Hispanics comprise about six per cent of the state's population, only about two per cent of the 11,500 students on campus are Hispanic, and as of 1991 the University had just one tenure-track Hispanic professor.

"We don't have a political base," Cardona said. "I was kind of amazed when I first came here from Nebraska, in 1985. Wyoming is so big and so spread out, people don't have a conception of the barriers we face. One of the big problems is we don't have enough network systems in this state.

"Wyoming is so isolated—and we have many students who don't realize the minority presence in the state, or they think it isn't significant. There's also this attitude that "We don't have to learn about other people, because we don't have them in Wyoming." People who have grown up in a rural area may never have seen a non-Anglo until they came to the University. All they know about diversity is what they see on TV.

"Demographics are changing, but the implications have not hit home. We do have a lot of diversity in Wyoming. Among the Hispanics, you'll find it all in this state—people from Mexico, people from Central and South America, people who are Mexican-American coming up from Texas and Mexico, people from New Mexico and Colorado.

"Within the Hispanic community there's classism. People who have roots in Colorado and New Mexico network like you wouldn't believe! They live here, but those ties are real strong and they travel back and forth a lot, too."

Delores Cardona believes people in Wyoming tend to judge people by who they are rather than by ethnic background.

Cardona said her parents came from Mexico to Texas, "through the migrant stream on up. My father was one of those who came north to find work." She believes she is the only Hispanic woman in Wyoming with a Ph.D. degree.

Hispanics settled along the future route of Interstate 80 during the late 1800s when they came to work on the railroad or in coal mines, Cardona said. They set up barrios near the railroad tracks in Cheyenne, Laramie, Rawlins, Rock Springs, and Green River.

"We have a real dearth of material written on us. A lot of times, when research is done on minorities, a lot of the research is urban. There's a real void of literature on the experience of minorities in rural areas." In the Multi-Cultural Center at the Student Union is a collection of oral histories of Hispanics in Wyoming, available to the public.

"A lot of minority students want to get the heck out of Wyoming after they graduate," Cardona said. "We have a minority brain drain, definitely. But we've had students come and like it here and stay, because this place is really laid back, and there's a quality of life here that attracts people.

"I've also seen people leave to go to a big city and come back. Often in rural areas the culture tends to be more vibrant because it is so isolated.

"There is a lot of work that needs to be done here. We have goals. We have increased minority enrollment at the university by over thirty percent since 1985. We have identified more than one hundred minority-oriented contacts within the state. A one-million-dollar fund has been set up for scholarships for Native Americans, and there are other scholarships for minority students in Cheyenne, Rawlins, and Casper.

"We have seven minority organizations on this campus. My predecessor originated an academic honor society, Epsilon, for non-traditional, minority, and low-income, disadvantaged students. I do believe it's unique.

"If you come here and you identify yourself as a minority, we will work with you and provide services."

⌁

Chapter 6

Laramie to Rawlins, I-80

ELK MOUNTAIN   *Population 174*
SINCLAIR   *Population 586*
*Question: Who was C. S. Bengough?

A Brief Background

From Laramie to Rawlins is ninety-nine miles via Interstate 80. You have a choice of three routes for the first seventy-seven miles, between Laramie and Walcott Junction. Interstate 80 is fastest, except during a snowstorm, when it is likely to be closed. The most scenic route is Highway 130 over the Snowy Range, through the Medicine Bow National Forest, but it stays open only during the summer and takes longer to travel. Highway 30, the old Lincoln Highway, is the most historical and best all-weather route, but it is seventeen miles longer than I-80.

Legend has it that the engineer who designed this stretch of Interstate 80 fell in love with the view from Elk Mountain and, against the advice of local residents, constructed the highway to include that view. The first week it opened, in October 1970, the highway closed because of blowing and drifting snow. It remained closed more than five percent of its first calendar year. Wyomingites sometimes refer to this route as the "Snow-Chi-Minh Trail."

These are a few landmarks along the I-80 route:

•• Arlington, which now has a campground for recreational vehicles, was once a way-station on the Overland Trail. Its main building was a combination store, dance hall, and school.

Here, in 1865, Arapaho Indians attacked a train of seventy-five wagons. They captured two young girls, Mary and Lizzie Fletcher, after killing their mother. A white trader bought Mary from the Arapahos a few months later and returned her to her father in Salt Lake City. Thirty-five years later a white woman raised as an Arapaho arrived in Casper with tribal members from the Wind River Reservation. Mary read about her, traveled to Casper to meet her, and identified her as her sister Lizzie. The woman shunned Mary and remained with her Arapaho family.

•• Elk Mountain is one of the prettiest towns along the Interstate. In the thirties its dance hall, the Garden Spot Pavilion, featured bands led by such notable musicians as Harry James, Louis Armstrong, and Tommy Dorsey. The hotel there was restored a few years ago.

•• A few miles past Walcott Junction is the turn-off for Fort Fred Steele, built to protect the Union Pacific Railroad. The fort has not been restored—only shells of old buildings remain. It is a wonderful place to go if you enjoy solitude.

•• Sinclair, once a company town called Parco, has lovely Spanish architecture, including a hotel which was restored with great expectations during the seventies—and then closed.

*Answer: C. S. Bengough was an Englishman whose family exiled him to Wyoming. His grave is on a hillside east of Interstate 80, two miles east of the Albany-Carbon County line. University of Wyoming students used to put flowers on his grave to bring them good luck on exams.

Chapter 7 – Laramie to Rawlins

Highway 130 Scenic Route

A beautiful alternate route from Laramie to Walcott is Highway 130 over the Snowy Range.

CENTENNIAL   *Population 50*
SARATOGA   *Population 1,969*
*Question: How did the town of Encampment get its name?

A Brief Background

Highway 130, over the Snowy Mountains, is a good two-lane road twelve thousand feet high at the summit. It usually opens in June and closes when the fall snows come. This isn't a fast route, but it is beautiful. The road was widened a few years ago and designated a National Scenic Byway.

Everything you could wish for in high-altitude forests you can find along 130: sparkling lakes, trout-filled streams, hiking trails, and even glaciers. You can usually see snow here all summer long. You have your choice of campgrounds close to the highway, but if you camp, be prepared for frigid night air.

Two towns border the Snowies along Highway 130: Centennial on the eastern slope, and Saratoga to the west. Some out-of-towners visit these communities just for their restaurants. Both towns have fine museums, but Centennial's is open only on Saturday and Sunday afternoons. Sculptor

Robert Russin lives in Centennial. James Michener visited Centennial in 1976 and autographed copies of his book by that name, although he said he didn't have the town in mind when he chose his title.

If you have time, after you cross the Snowies, detour thirteen miles south to Encampment (population 490) before heading north to Saratoga. Encampment is an old-time copper-mining community with one of the most popular history museums in Wyoming. A memorable feature is its two-story outhouse. When deep snow buried the first story, the top story was put into use.

The world's largest aerial tramway, sixteen miles long, connected a smelter at Encampment with the Ferris-Haggerty copper mine. Rudefeha and Dillon, ghost towns now, were established near that mine. Dillon originated because the mine managers banned liquor sales in Rudefeha. Dillon's population soon surpassed its dry neighbor's.

Grant Jones, founder of the weekly *Dillon Doublejack*, wrote newspaper columns about mythical animals such as the Coogly Woo, the Bockaboar, and the One-Eyed Screaming Emu. Jones was an alcoholic. When he missed one week's newspaper deadline, he reprinted the paper from the week before, declaring that "we've had so many compliments on last week's issue...we're delighted to run it again this week."

The town of Riverside (population 85) adjoins Encampment, and the two communities share services.

The North Platte River runs through Saratoga, twenty-one miles north of Encampment, and townspeople boast that "the trout leap in Main Street." The Wyoming Game and Fish Department has designated this section of the North Platte as a blue-ribbon trout stream. A fish hatchery is five miles north of town.

Apart from fishing, Saratoga's main attraction is its mineral hot springs and waters, nicknamed Hobo Pool. Native Americans used to bathe in the hot springs until 1874. In that year they tried to cure victims of smallpox, a disease spread by white settlers, by dipping their patients in the hot water to boil out the sickness and then into the cold river. Patients died, and their caretakers decided then that the mineral hot springs were bad medicine.

The Town of Saratoga now maintains the pool, with changing rooms and showers, free to the public.

Saratoga has one of Wyoming's two oldest hotels. The Wolf Hotel and restaurant, built in 1893, is a designated National Historic Landmark.

Timber has been important to Saratoga's economy. Until 1938 the Union Pacific Railroad bought hand-hewn ties, eight feet long and eleven inches in diameter. Tie hacks cut them from lodgepole pines. In the spring they floated the ties downstream to a treatment plant at Fort Fred Steele.

To learn more about tie hacks, visit the Saratoga museum or take a walking history tour of tie hack camps in the Sierra Madre and Medicine Bow Mountains, led by the U. S. Forest Service.

To rejoin Interstate 80, drive twenty miles north on Highway 130 to Walcott Junction. You will then be twenty-two miles east of Rawlins, where the Red Desert begins.

ᴕ

*Answer: Encampment was named for the Grand Encampment, an annual rendezvous of fur traders, trappers, and Native Americans during the mid-1800s.

About the Close-Up

•• You have probably noticed Robert Russin's statues in Cheyenne, at the Interstate summit, and in Laramie. Now the artist talks about his work and answers the question, What is Western art?

Close-up: Robert Russin

About twenty years ago the Casper Chamber of Commerce asked Robert Russin to make a bucking horse statue for the front of its office building. Russin responded: "I can do that. The question is, do you do that and milk it to death? There are so many bucking horses all over Wyoming, what would be so special about a bucking horse in Casper? What Casper is about is energy."

Russin created for the Chamber of Commerce *Man and Energy*, which he described as "global man looking within himself at the energy he is trying to create and the problems that are breaking his world apart."

"It's a very somber statue—it's not a bucking horse at all," said Russin. "What I was trying to express was man's wish to contain the fragmented world.

"There's one thing to be constantly doing John Wayne over again in various interpretations, and another to be looking at contemporary man and at the way he lives. A lot of what passes for Western art today isn't Western art at all. The romantic West isn't here anymore—what it is is nostalgia.

"People who would not invite an Indian off the reservation into their homes will buy a painting of a mythical noble Indian and feel good about it," said Russin. "If you're falling back to what people would like to think because there's money in it, that's not an artistic endeavor at all.

"Western art should be whatever is here now. That means all the problems that society faces—that you and I face. There isn't any reason we're not as beautiful as a cowboy or an Indian. We're part of the West, and that is what Western art should be.

Robert Russin sculpted several works along I-80, including this mountain man found at Cheyenne's Travel Information Center. He lives in Centennial, Wyoming, between Laramie and Rawlins.

"The other part of Western art is the feeling for nature and for our beautiful sky. We have a very sharp, penetrating light, with very little dust in the air. It's clear, brilliant, special— unmatched in most places in the world."

In the Herschler Building in Cheyenne hangs a giant crystal which Russin completed during the eighties. "That's the crystal of carbon. Carbon is the basis of economic wealth in this state. It just happens that the crystal of carbon is the same crystal as that of the diamond, so I chose that as a symbol.

It's in an atrium, so when the sun passes over, it changes color constantly. Everything a diamond does, it does. I did it in clear plastic acrylic to capture the clarity of the sky, which is a beautiful part of living in Wyoming.

"Between the parts I used dicroic filter, often used in outer space, to filter certain wave lengths of light and reflect all the others. All of those are refracted through the shape of the diamond. I wanted to capture some of that marvelous color that you get in Wyoming. In my mind, that's a Western sculpture."

Russin, a native New Yorker, moved his family to Centennial in 1947 in hopes that the dry Wyoming climate would curb his wife's and son's asthma. For many years he was art professor and Artist-in Residence at the University of Wyoming, and he has recently been named Distinguished Professor, an honor bestowed upon only one per cent of faculty retirees. The university held a retrospective exhibit of Russin's art during Homecoming 1991.

Russin's public sculptures stand in New York, Pennsylvania, Illinois, Kansas, Colorado, Texas, Arizona, California, Washington D.C. and Santo Domingo, as well as in Wyoming. He recently completed a monument to the Holocaust for the Jewish Community Center in Tucson, Arizona.

He said he has a few favorites among his Wyoming works. One is his bust of Lincoln on the I-80 summit. "I'm drawn back to Lincoln on the hill because I admire the man so much. I always think, 'Could I have done it better?' and I'd like to do it again.

"I'm very fond of the *University Family* up on the campus because that seems to be a good symbol of the melding of family members, of family members reaching out to each other. In the end, that's the essential. Some attention to the beauty of family growth is a worthwhile artistic and sculptural endeavor. While it's been done many times, it's always rewarding to do it freshly.

"*Prometheus*, at the library up in Casper, seems to be a good symbol of knowledge, which man is always searching for, and of the difficulty of obtaining it."

Russin's sculpture has brought him many honors—and only a few detractors. Most harsh was the sheepherder who came into the bar at the Park Hotel in Rock Springs and viewed one of Russin's earliest Wyoming works, a plastic wildlife mobile. "He didn't like the mobile, and he'd had a little too much to drink," said Russin. "So he pulled out a rifle and shot it!"

A granite statue of man and energy stands at the entrance to the Department of Energy in Washington D.C. "For me, that's another Western statue. I took the forms of exfoliated granite that you find around Casper, in the mountains. It shows the splitting apart of the earth because of the development of atomic energy. The ultimate thing is destruction if man doesn't solve his problems.'

"Here [in Wyoming] wagons came one hundred years ago over the Overland Trail—and we have missile sites in Cheyenne. Here we are in dead center danger of being attacked because we have missile sites right here. We're not removed from the world, we're pinpointed. That's all part of today's West."

Highway 30 Historic Route

If time allows, consider leaving I-80 at Laramie and taking Highway 30 until it reconnects with I-80 at Walcott. This detour is rich in history and folklore.

BOSLER   *Population, rumored as 9*
ROCK RIVER   *Population, 190*
MEDICINE BOW   *Population, 389*
HANNA   *Population, 1,076*

*Question: Who said, "When you call me that, smile!"

A Brief Background

Bosler and Rock River WERE thriving towns with motels, restaurants, and service stations before Interstate 80 by-passed them in 1970. Bosler has just one business now, Doc's Western Village, a sprawling discount furniture store and used car lot. The public school closed a few years ago.

Long-time area residents say that a ghost lived in Bosler during the 1920s and 1930s. During the early 1980s Pat McGuire, who owned a ranch near Bosler on Sybille Canyon Road, reported that extraterrestrial beings visited him and told him where to dig his irrigation well. McGuire followed their recommendation, even though hydrologists advised him not to, and his well became the highest producing water well west of the Mississippi, according to local lore. After McGuire left his ranch, the well ran dry.

During the early 1980s a topless bar opened in Bosler, to the dismay of the town's few remaining citizens. The performers came from Denver. For a few weeks the bar drew curious customers from neighboring towns—and then it closed.

If you were to detour twenty-six miles up Sybille Canyon Road (State Highway 34), you would come to the wildlife center where black-footed ferrets are cared for. A colony of the nearly-extinct creatures was discovered near Meeteetse, in northwestern Wyoming, in 1981. Unfortunately, most of the ferrets there died of a plague, perhaps spread by fleas from a researcher's dog, so most of the surviving ferrets were moved to the Sybille Canyon center. After the population of ferrets at the center increased, some were released onto ranches near Shirley Basin, north of Medicine Bow.

Ferrets are nocturnal animals. You can watch them sleeping, via television monitor, if you visit the center.

Rock River has more residents than Bosler, and its school is still operating, thanks in part to students who commute thirty-nine miles from Laramie to take advantage of Rock River's small classes. When the high school's five seniors graduated in May, 1990, Governor Mike Sullivan gave the commencement address.

A few miles north of Rock River, Butch Cassidy and his gang pulled off a spectacular train robbery in 1899. Six masked men flagged down the train, dynamited the baggage and express cars, and escaped with thousands in bills and bank notes.

A Hollywood film crew arrived at Rock River in 1917 to make *The Man from Painted Post*, starring Douglas Fairbanks Sr. But when local ranchers caught sight of actors wearing chaps—dyed pink, because that color showed up best on black and white film—they ran the movie folks off. *The Man from Painted Post* was eventually made at Jelm, southwest of Laramie.

Dinosaurs roamed Wyoming more than one hundred million years ago. At that time the land was near sea level and was covered with lush vegetation. After the land folded and rose to its present elevation, seven thousand feet, dinosaur bones and fossils lay near the surface at Como Bluff. Como Bluff is an anticline (upfolding of strata) about ten miles long and one mile wide, northwest of Rock River.

Two Union Pacific Railroad employees first discovered the fossils in 1877. They wrote to Professor Othniel Charles Marsh at the Yale Peabody Museum, who sent his field assistant, Samuel Williston, to meet with them. Williston found that the number and diversity of bones at Como Bluff far exceeded those in any other sites where Marsh had sent crews.

The workers Professor Marsh sent to Como Bluff uncovered twenty-six new species of dinosaur, many with complete or nearly complete skeletons, and forty-five new species of mammals from the Jurassic period. Their collection included an Apatosaurus (Brontosaurus) more than sixty-five feet long, now at the University of Wyoming's Geology Museum. (Scientists have since determined that the skull actually belonged to a different dinosaur, Camarasaurias.) An eighty-seven-and-one-half-foot skeleton of a Diplodocus, the largest dinosaur known, was also discovered at Como Bluff and is on display at Carnegie Tech University in Pittsburgh, Pennsylvania.

Marsh's arch-rival, Professor Edward Dunker Cope of the Philadelphia Academy of Science, also sent crews to Como Bluff. Hostilities between Marsh's and Cope's workers led to fist fights, rock throwing and bone smashing. Marsh achieved revenge in part by giving fossilized dinosaur manure Cope's name.

If you drive seven miles north on Marshall Road, west of Rock River, you will come close to the original Como Bluff site. It is on private property, and nothing in its appearance distinguishes it from the surrounding land—unless you happen to be a paleontologist.

The region drew widespread attention again in 1990, when two Colorado high school science teachers made new dinosaur bone discoveries there. The teachers contacted University of Colorado paleontologist Robert Bakker, who brought a crew to the site and set up summer headquarters in Rock River. Bakker is providing some reconstructions of fossils from the site to the Rock River Museum.

About twelve miles west of Rock River stands a cabin said to be the oldest in the world because it is made from dinosaur bones—twenty-six thousand pieces of fossil from the nearby bluff. You can see it from the highway, and if the owners are home, you can pay them a dollar and view the displays inside.

Highway 30 goes right through downtown Medicine Bow, a town whose population dropped from 953 in 1980, to 389 ten years later. Medicine Bow stood in the center of a multiple-industry area, with uranium mines at Shirley Basin to the north, coal mines at Hanna to the west, several ranches, a Bureau of Reclamation wind project, and summer tourists.

But during the eighties the uranium and most coal mines closed, several small ranches were merged into large ones with absentee owners, and the wind project shut down after the federal government withdrew funds. The die-hard Medicine Bow citizens who remain welcome tourists.

In summer the museum in the old Union Pacific depot is a good starting point. You can picnic at the table outside. A board showing the brands of area ranches, signs relating to Owen Wister's cowboy novel, *The Virginian*, and Wister's summer cabin stand nearby. *The Virginian's* first three chapters are set in Medicine Bow. Across the highway is Medicine Bow's showcase hotel—named, of course, The Virginian. The Diplodocus, down the street, has the longest bar in the world made from jade, plus wood carvings created by the bar's owner. An art gallery opened in Medicine Bow in 1992.

Medicine Bow's name comes from the mountain range surrounding the town. Indians came to the Medicine Bow Mountains to gather ash wood for bows and arrows. They held ceremonial dances to cure diseases. Both the dances and the wood were "good medicine."

Hanna, the last town between Laramie and Walcott Junction, is a coal mining community built by the Union Pacific Railroad in 1889. Some fatal mining accidents happened here—four in 1892 alone. In 1893, miners rebelled. Two hundred of them marched into the Union Pacific superintendent's office and declared that if the mine boss didn't leave town within twenty-four hours, they would hang him. The mine boss left.

The worst mining disaster in Wyoming history happened in Hanna on June 30, 1902, when 169 miners died in an explosion. One hundred fifty women were widowed; six hundred children lost their fathers as a result of that accident. They lost not only their loved ones and their income but also their homes, since the only houses available for miners were owned by Union Pacific. Widows couldn't take over their dead spouses' jobs because the law prohibited women from working in mines. Five years later fifty-nine miners died at Hanna when two explosions occurred the same day.

In 1954 the Union Pacific closed Hanna's coal mines. Some mines opened during the seventies, and a few are still operating. You can see them from the highway, off to the right, just before you come to the Hanna turn-off. A memorial in Hanna honors miners who have been killed on the job.

The monument photo shows two granite markers. The left reads:

DEDICATED TO ALL COAL MINERS IN THE CARBON—HANNA AREA IN MEMORY OF THOSE WHO LOST THEIR LIVES IN MINING ACCIDENTS

The right lists names by year (1916–1972), including THOMAS UKOLA, H BAROUXAKIS, MATT UKKOLA, JOE MORRIS, MERLE MILLER, and others.

This monument in Hanna honors miners who have lost their lives in coal mine accidents in the Hanna area.

*Answer: The Virginian said "When you call me that, smile!" to Trampas, the villain, in Chapter Two of Wister's novel, after Trampas called him "you son of a ___" during a card game.

About the Close-Ups

•• If John Guthrie has his way, Rock River will have a major dinosaur museum, and tourists will flock here to take part in the Highway 30 Experience.

•• Bill Young knew, when he bought the world's largest wind turbine, repairing it wouldn't be easy. What really riled him was our government's disregard for the benefits of wind power.

•• Steve Kesy and Keith Black were coal miners at Hanna during the eighties, and they show us what modern-day coal mining is like.

••If you stop in Medicine Bow, you will see plenty of memorabilia of Owen Wister's novel, *The Virginian*. Who was Owen Wister anyway, and how did this Eastern lawyer come to write the first successful cowboy novel?

••Meet David Roberts: author of *Sage Street*, co-author of *Wyoming Almanac*, newspaper publisher, teacher, philosopher—and more. David, a native Wyomingite, no longer lives in Medicine Bow. The conversation in the close-up took place in 1984.

Close-Up: JOHN GUTHRIE

HE SAYS HE HAS BEEN CALLED "the Andy Warhol of the West," and his paintings hang in more than twenty galleries.

John Guthrie III worked as a commercial photographer in Australia and as a documentary film cameraman in Asia and the Soviet Union. He produced a television documentary on the space industry that won the Eric Sevareid Award and wrote and produced the film *Earthwalk*, narrated by Orson Welles.

He wrote a book about manned, hypersonic space flight and created and marketed a satellite-delivered news graphics service.

So what brings John Guthrie III to Rock River, Wyoming? He grew up in Laramie, and in 1988 he started creating "Far West" paintings, which, he said, "reflect the frontier spirit that is part of everyone's heritage, regardless of where they are from." He bought a three-unit apartment building in Rock River for ten thousand dollars, which serves as his home, studio, and office.

Shortly after he moved there, Guthrie made a startling observation. "Rock River is dying, and anybody who doesn't think so is whistling by the graveyard."

To revive his town, Guthrie devised the Highway 30 Experience, a campaign to promote tourism in Rock River and Medicine Bow. Guthrie presented slide shows and gave talks urging local citizens to join his campaign. They responded skeptically at first, then caught Guthrie's enthusiasm and agreed to give his ideas a try.

John Guthrie wants Rock River to be the home of a major dinosaur museum and a stop on the Highway 30 Experience.

But by the summer of 1991, plans for the only tourist attraction proposed for Rock River—a dinosaur museum—had come to a standstill. "Nobody really knows what the next thing is to do," said Guthrie. "My original concept was you'd have dinosaurs in Rock River and the romance of the Old West in Medicine Bow. But the people in town don't want me to be the director—I'm too radical. They're just kind of stalled."

Guthrie envisioned that Rock River's museum would show dinosaur discoveries from Como Bluff. Then he would produce an audio-cassette tape for tourists to play as they drove from Laramie, to Rock River, to Medicine Bow, "so the whole thing would be marketed as an experience.

"Our primary market would be Denver. Secondary markets would be Cheyenne, Laramie, and special interest groups. The Highway 30 Experience would hand off at Medicine Bow to the Natrona County Experience for those heading north to Casper."

The promotion would spread to include all of Wyoming, Guthrie said. The state could then franchise the idea and set up a cottage industry, paying residents to mail out instructions to Chambers of Commerce all across the United States on how to adapt the Highway 30 Experience to their towns.

The people of Rock River did take the first step—investing in a new roof for the former bank chosen to be the museum. And the Albany County Tourism Board promised to pay for Guthrie's billboard of a cowgirl riding a pink dinosaur, directing visitors to the museum two blocks from the highway. Guthrie painted another advertising billboard in Laramie.

"I say 'Let's grow; let's do something; let's be something here that has a chance,'" Guthrie said. "But the people of Rock River have to want to save themselves. If they don't want this, I don't want to apply for state grants."

The Highway 30 Experience may have come too late for Rock River. The town's only restaurant closed, even while plans were in the making to promote the town. The school was having to recruit pupils from Laramie because it didn't have enough local ones. The town had no ambulance, no paramedics, no health facilities.

"It can't go on like this; it'll die," Guthrie said. "I've had so many people tell me 'Rock River will always be here.'

"And I say, 'Is that right? Where are your children? Where are your grandchildren?' They move away, because there's no way to make a living here.

"I'm 38. As the baby boom generation moves into middle age, we're going to reassert some values that have been lacking in our lives, and a lot of us are fed up with the cities. But there has to be something for us to come back to.

"I'm afraid Wyoming will turn into a zoo. People will come here to look at the wildlife and then go back to Colorado, where the jobs are."

The Highway 30 Experience isn't Rock River's only possibility for survival, Guthrie admits. A Utah firm may build an elaborate visitors' center near the dinosaur fossil cabin at Como Bluff. And the area surrounding Rock River has a rare asset—an extremely pure grade of silica used for making fine china. A manufacturing plant might open here.

But these are mere possibilities, dependent on outside investors, whereas the museum is something Rock River citizens might develop themselves.

"I'm busy," Guthrie said. "If the people of Rock River don't want this, I can't waste my time on a losing cause."

Guthrie's art keeps him busy. In July, 1991, he invested twelve hundred dollars and a good deal of time painting *Tom Mix Transcending the Veil* on the screen of Laramie's former drive-in movie—a painting which he removed a year later rather than keep paying liability insurance in case it distracted a driver and caused an accident. Smaller paintings by Guthrie hang in Laramie's Third Street Bar and Grill.

"I don't think of myself as an artist," said Guthrie. "I'm becoming an artist, and I'll be a great artist someday. But right now, I'm just a very creative businessman."

Update: The Rock River museum opened in 1992. It contains fossils and historical artifacts donated by local citizens. Volunteers serve at the museum during the summer. As of 1993, Dr. Bakker was rebuilding a reconstruction of a fossil found at Como Bluff to fit the museum space. The restaurant, motel, and convenience store also reopened. In 1993 John Guthrie founded a telephone company offering calling cards for travelers and planned to make Rock River the company's global headquarters. He remains active in the museum.

Close-Up: BILL YOUNG

NINE HOURS A DAY HE worked alone, in cramped quarters, using instruments the size of dental tools. Bill Young's workplace was two hundred sixty-two feet above the prairie, five miles southwest of Medicine Bow. His goal was to get the world's most powerful wind turbine running again.

The turbine cost eight million dollars when it was built in 1982. It broke down just before funding of the wind project was scheduled to be discontinued, so the U. S. Bureau of Reclamation sold the turbine rather than pay for repairs. Only two people offered to buy it. Young's twenty thousand dollar bid was high.

Young was no Don Quixote. He was construction site engineer for the Medicine Bow wind project, and he knew the workings of the machine he purchased better than anyone else. The turbine stopped running because a half-inch bolt snapped, throwing the generator out of sync and causing damage to some copper coils. Rewinding the coils would cost two hundred thousand dollars.

"We did a number of repairs that cost more than that when the turbine was running" he said. "We probably spent half a million fixing a yaw problem in the summer of 1983. I'm poor-boying the job" Young said, in 1991. "I don't quite have two hundred thousand dollars this week. I'm hoping to get it repaired for twenty thousand dollars."

He eliminated the six damaged coils by cutting them out of the electrical circuit. He also repaired the stator iron, an eighteen-month chore.

"Now I'm repairing a rotor. I'm finding it's taking a little longer than I expected. It was a bolt on the rotor that caused the failure. I'm trying to reduce the chances of its happening again by putting in stronger bolts and doing a better job of putting them in than the factory that built them."

Young said the turbine, the Hamilton-Standard-WTS-4, would generate four megawatts of electricity, enough to supply sixteen hundred households, once it was running again. It weighs four hundred tons, and when its blades are in vertical position, they reach a height of three hundred ninety-one feet. The foundation extends seventy feet into the ground.

Young said he wasn't in any hurry to finish the repairs. "If there's a lot of money involved, people are always in a hurry to get things done. In my case, I'm retired, and I don't have that kind of pressure. My inclination is not to rush through things. It's worth it, spending more time on the details to get things right."

Another reason he wasn't in a rush is there was no market for wind power in Wyoming. "The utilities in this area over-built with coal-generating plants in the seventies and eighties. They're offering the second lowest-priced power in the United States. Nobody wants my wind power. I'll be lucky to half-give it away, Young lamented in 1991."

A plant in Wheatland produces fifteen hundred megawatts of electric power, Young said, and the Jim Bridger Power Plant at Point of Rocks along Interstate 80 produces two thousand megawatts, more than the area needs. The Jim Bridger Plant sells power to California.

"It isn't just economics, it's [federal] politics," said Young. "We don't have a transportation policy, we don't have an energy policy, we don't have any policies that make sense.

"Disaster struck on the twenty-second of January of 1981, when Ronald Reagan was sworn in as President. The [alternative energy] budget was slashed every year after that until it was down to nine million dollars. The interest just dried up for the wind program, and they let it die.

"I think the government was wrong—dead wrong. We're already paying eighty dollars a barrel for Mideast oil, if you

Bill Young bought the world's largest wind turbine, when the Bureau of Reclamation couldn't keep it running, and put it into production.

figure aid to countries like Egypt and our military presence throughout the Middle East. And that's without Desert Storm!

"We're letting public transportation disintegrate while we pour money into highways, while the railroads go to hell. Do you know how much more it costs to haul by truck than to ship by train? Six times as much!

"We won't electrify railroads to get them off oil because we're too dumb—we're looking only at the immediate dollars.

"We could save a tremendous portion of the energy we use in the United States just through conservation. We could save twenty percent of our electrical energy—the entire output of nuclear plants in this country—just by designing buildings so they didn't use so much power.

"I've been working in renewable energy my whole career with the Bureau of Reclamation. I worked with hydro-electric power since 1957. I went into it because it was renewable energy. Hydro-electric power provides twelve percent of the power in the U.S.—but there's only so much available."

The Medicine Bow wind project tied in with hydro-electric power. Reservoirs behind regional dams were to serve as energy batteries, storing potential power when the wind was blowing and generating power when the wind stopped.

"Of all the solar power available, wind is the cheapest," said Young. He believes so strongly in wind power, he even bought the substation from a turbine the government had demolished, and "badgered the government into letting us keep it on the property. I saved it, hoping that somebody would want to put up a wind farm here with state-of-the-art machines."

The government once planned for twenty-five wind turbines near Medicine Bow generating one hundred megawatts of power, Young said. Medicine Bow is said to be the second windiest town in the United States.

Young worked on, alone on the prairie, even though nobody offered to buy his wind power. "I wouldn't be doing it if I didn't enjoy it. After so many hours it gets kind of old, though. Physically, you get kind of stove up. I have to sit with one leg bent, and pretty soon you realize you'd better straighten your leg or you won't be able to."

He said if he had it to do over, knowing what he knew then he would still purchase the Hamilton-Standard WTS-4. "There haven't been any big surprises. It's taking maybe a little longer than I anticipated, but that's the way things always run.

"All I can say is sometime I hope to market wind power. I'd like it to be in the near future—we have very good wind."

Bill Young's tenacity paid off. In 1992 his financial partners Glidden Doman, invested sixty thousand dollars to complete repairs on the wind turbine. Since November 1992, Young has been selling electricity to Western Area Power Administration at 1.8 cents per kilowatt-hour.

Several companies have also expressed interest in establishing a wind farm near Medicine Bow.

Close-Up: STEVE KESY AND KEITH BLACK

IN 1973, WHEN HE WAS eighteen, Steve Kesy came west from Wisconsin. He panned gold, worked on oil rigs, did a little welding, set charges in bentonite fields, and swept parking lots at bars. He hitchhiked wherever he went until one of his bosses gave him a car, a 1964 Chrysler.

"Everybody was just real transient," Kesy said. "The work was so available, people just did it for a little while and moved on to something else."

He went to Cheyenne. "There was hardly any work there. It seemed like all the jobs were in real remote, desolate places."

Kesy moved to Shirley Basin, north of Medicine Bow, and worked at a uranium strip mine. There he met the woman he would later marry, who was also a miner. He stayed at Shirley Basin five years.

"All I did was haul off the overburden—the dirt that lies over the uranium," said Kesy. "I drove this one-hundred-twenty-ton truck. It was so big, you could put six cars in it. I had to walk up a ladder to get to the cab. When I stood on the ground, my head came level with the hub of the wheel. It was just so massive, you'd look at it and think. 'God, how could anybody drive this?' But the fastest it would go was twenty-one miles an hour. It was the easiest job I had. Then the bottom fell out of the uranium market and the mine closed down."

A coal miner knocks down porous coal with a twenty-foot pole. (Keith Black photo)

He went to Hanna then and mined coal. "I was really reluctant, because it was an underground mine. I thought it was the very last thing I would ever do in my life, but there was no more work on oil rigs, and the railroads were laying off. It was the very last job I had an offer for."

Keith Black went to work at a Hanna coal mine in 1978 and stayed a little more than a year. That mine has since closed. "They shut down because there were too many accidents," he said. "Towards the end there were deaths. There was a cave-in where three men were killed. It was my crew— but I was gone. They were mining in an area that had been sealed off because it was so hazardous, but the foreman wanted that coal. The managers were greedy; they didn't think about safety.

"There was lots of turnover. If you didn't like it, leave. They didn't care if you got killed; they didn't care if you left.

Keith Black, once a coal miner in Hanna, now owns a photography studio in Cheyenne.

You'd just suck up coal dust, but I didn't see a respirator the whole time I was there.

"They used to use dynamite, and I'd get to set the charges. That was real weird. You'd be real close, and you'd have to holler 'Fire in the hole!' three times before you set it off. You'd stay in the cross-cut to protect yourself. The first few times it went off you'd go, 'Oh God, it's all over!' Then you'd have to go in and see that all the blasting caps had gone off before anyone could get back in there."

After he left that mine, Black went to work at the uranium mine at Shirley Basin, where he met Kesy. When it closed in 1981, he hired on with the same coal company that Kesy did.

⚹

Wyoming coal mines employ both room-and-pillar and long-wall mining. Room-and-pillar means leaving large columns of coal intact to serve as supports in the "rooms" where the miners are working. In long-wall mining, the

Both miners agree that coal mining is dangerous work. Here a woman miner sets an explosive charge. (Keith Black photo)

workers remove all the coal, and use wooden props and brick and rubble "pack walls" to support the undermined areas.

"You'd make a cut twenty feet wide, then cross cuts, then another entry," said Black. "You'd put timbers up. They would pull the pillars. You'd just hope you could get out of there before everything caved in."

"We were mining in the side of a hill," Kesy said. "We drove in and out of the mine on tractors. They built cages on the back that would hold six people. We had people building walls, operating the miner, maintaining the cave-ins, bolting the roof.... I hired on as a welder, but I walked the belt for about six months. We had to keep the fine spills of coal off the ground. Everything had to be shoveled by hand. I lost forty pounds. I figure I carried around seventy pounds of equipment, walking up and down hill shoveling all day.

"Later I worked on a dead shift as a mechanic. Before the crew would come in I'd have to go in with a methane detector and get a reading at different levels. You couldn't energize anything if there was gas in there. I never detected any gas.

"We did have black damp—dead air. You walk into it, it knocks you out. I'd carry a safety lamp and check for it.

"When you cut coal, it sucks air like crazy because it's so porous. After awhile it forms big cracks and topples over. So you really have to watch it. If it got that bad, you were supposed to get a bar twenty feet long and knock it down. Nobody wanted to do it.

"A lot of times we had cave-ins. I was in a section where the roof caved in. It was like nothing I'd ever seen before. The coal was so big, we were there with sledge hammers for two weeks breaking it up. Luckily, nobody got hurt.

"One person was seriously hurt when a rib [wall] fell down and squashed him. He was a young guy, in great physical shape, and that just destroyed his life.

"The people I worked with were safety-conscious. The company gave us safety equipment—respirators, ear plugs and safety glasses. Everybody was good about warning each other about danger, even if you didn't like the person. There were people who took shortcuts and they got fired for it, because they put everybody in their crew in danger.

"You always worked in pairs. There was a lot of camaraderie. The oldest guy there was forty-something, the youngest eighteen or nineteen. Most of us were in our twenties.

"Coal dust is real explosive, so you'd go in and rock dust the areas to keep the fire hazard down," Black said. "I did that for quite awhile. And then I drove a diesel truck. You'd be driving at breakneck speed because they wanted you to push it just as fast as you could go. And you were working in the return air, the bad air that was coming out of the mine— the coal dust, the exhaust. With the diesel fumes, the dust,

Rock-dusting helps to keep the dust in the coal mine from exploding. (Keith Black photo)

sometimes you couldn't see your hands in front of your face. I'd be throwing up all the time. I just couldn't handle it.

"In the winter it was real cold. The heaters weren't working half the time. When you have that much air circulating—the heaters were just constantly breaking."

"Right at the mouth of the mine it would get fifty below," Kesy said. "You'd drive out of the mine and it would be so cold coming up against your face, it would give you headaches.

"The mines were really wet; you were always wading in water. When it rained, I've seen waves coming down the intakes three feet tall. Then everyone had a hard time getting out, because the roads were slick. The tension would get pretty high sometimes. There'd be fights underground.

"It was really back-breaking work, and you'd come out just black, it was so dirty. Our eyes would look like we were wearing mascara, and we'd have black in our pores. Our fingernails were always dirty."

"To me it was just a dirty, nasty job where you were dirty all the time," Black said. "They didn't have a good water purification system, so even the water we took showers in was dirty."

"Some people couldn't deal with the danger," Kesy said.

"I liked the danger; I hated the job," said Black.

Said Kesy: "There were mice in the mine, and bats. If somebody was jumpy all the time, we'd put mice in their lunchbox."

Keith Black left this coal mine after a year and a half and now owns the Photo Album in Cheyenne. Steve Kesy mined coal five years.

"I thought my life was pretty well set as a miner," said Kesy. "I could make forty thousand dollars a year—better, putting in overtime. There was no other place I could make that money. I was interviewing with Arm & Hammer to go to China as a miner. They would have paid me a hundred thousand dollars a year."

Kesy made enough money mining to help pay his wife's way through law school, and she is now a lawyer at the attorney general's office in Cheyenne.

Kesy's mining career ended when he had a serious auto accident commuting eighty miles to Laramie. He broke both legs, his back, his neck, and his ribs, and punctured his lungs. Miraculously, he has nearly recovered—but he can no longer mine coal. He enrolled in Laramie County Community College and then the University of Wyoming.

"Mining was like nothing I'd ever done before," Kesy said. "There was something about the atmosphere—people

Steve Kesy left mining following a serious automobile accident. He had intended to make mining a lifetime career.

were always watching out for everybody. There was always that constant fear that I'd get caught in a cave-in, though, and that really bothered me."

Close-Up: OWEN WISTER

ON JULY 19, 1885, OWEN WISTER rode ninety miles on horse-back into Medicine Bow with his rancher-host, Major Wolcott, to pick up a shipment of fish for Walcott's pond. Wister slept on the counter of the general store for a few hours while waiting for the shipment to arrive by train.

But first, he took inventory of Medicine Bow: "One depot and baggage room, one coal shooter, one water tank, one store, two eating houses, one billiard hall, six shanties, eight gents' and ladies' walks, two tool houses, one feed stable, and five buildings too late for classification."

"I have walked nearly two acres in order to carefully ascertain the exact details of this town, and I feel assured my returns are correct," Wister wrote in a letter home.

Years later, when Wister wrote *The Virginian* he set the first three chapters in Medicine Bow.

Wister's first summer in Wyoming changed the course of his life. He was on the verge of a nervous breakdown when he rode the Union Pacific from Philadelphia to visit Major Walcott's ranch.

Wister had majored in music at Harvard and had hoped to become a composer, but his father, a physician, squelched young Wister's dreams. He wanted his twenty-five-year-old son to follow a "respectable" occupation that wouldn't embarrass the family, so he arranged for Owen to work at the Union Safe Deposit Vaults in Boston, computing interest. Wister's disappointment and frustration caused his health to fail, and his uncle, also a physician, suggested the trip west as a tonic. The journey succeeded beyond anyone's expectations.

The Wyoming landscape exhilarated Wister, just as music had. He compared the scenery to passages by Wagner: "Those moments when the whole orchestra seems to break into silver fragments of magic—sounds of harps and violins all away up somewhere, sustaining some theme you have heard before, but which now returns twice as magnificent... those passages are inspired by the same thing which vibrates in this canyon."

But Wister called Western towns "a wretched husk of squalor." He wrote to his mother, "The only way you could come West and enjoy yourself would be inside a large party of friends who would form a hollow space whenever a public place was to be entered."

In Chapter Two of *The Virginian* Wister described Wyoming towns in this manner: "They lay stark, dotted over a planet of treeless dust, like soiled packs of cards.... More forlorn they were than stale bones. They seemed to have been strewn there by the wind and to be waiting till the wind should come again and blow them away."

At the end of the summer Wister entered Harvard Law School. But he returned to Wyoming each summer for the next fourteen years, usually bringing along some friends. Not until 1891, while dining with a friend who also loved the West, did Wister decide to write about Wyoming. He recorded in his journal:

> From oysters to coffee we compared experiences. Why wasn't some Kipling saving the sagebrush for American literature before the sagebrush and all it signified went the way of the forty-niner, went the way of the Mississippi steam boat, went the way of everything?
>
> "Walter! I'm going to try it myself!" I exclaimed. "I'm going to start this minute."

He wrote most of the short story "Hank's Woman" that night and sold it and a second short story to *Harper's* Magazine.

The Virginian (who is never called by any other name) made his first appearance as a minor character in "Hank's Woman" and appeared again in Wister's first book, *Lin McLean*, published in 1895. McLean, a young cowboy, can't understand the Virginian's patience in courting the prudish New England schoolmarm, Molly Wood. "If all the girls were that chilly, why, what would us poor punchers do? Has she promised to be your sister yet?" he asks the Virginian.

Lin McLean came closer to fitting Wister's image of the typical cowboy than the Virginian did. "I'm told they're

Medicine Bow is home to the Virginian Hotel which was built in 1911, nine years after Owen Wister's famous novel was published.

without any moral sense whatever," Wister wrote in his journal in 1885.

Some western critics today call the Virginian more Eastern capitalist than Wyoming cowboy. "I'm the kind who moves up," he assures his beloved Molly Wood. And move up he does, becoming foreman and then owner of his own ranch. He even invests in a coal mine.

The Virginian found instant popularity; it went through fifteen reprintings in the first eight months following publication in 1902. It has been made into a movie three times, with Dustin Farnum, Gary Cooper, and Joel McCrea playing the title role. For twenty years a play based on Wister's novel played in summer stock, and for several seasons a television series carried the name.

Wister's daughter, Fanny Kemble Stokes, wrote in 1958: "For the first time, a cowboy was a gentleman and a hero...

hundreds of young girls fell in love with him. Before then, cowboys had been depicted as murderous thugs."

In reminiscing about his life as a cowboy in the eighteen nineties, Bruce Siberts wrote: "I had a liking for the girls, but when I went into town with my rough clothes on, they wouldn't pay attention to me.... Owen Wister hadn't yet written his book *The Virginian*, so we cowhands did not know we were so strong and glamorous as we were after people read that book."

We don't know how many teachers came West in hopes of finding a Virginian to marry. According to *Cow Belles Ring School Bells,* rural Wyoming teachers "were often looking for two things: a job and a prospective husband."

Wana Clay Olson, once Albany County, Wyoming Superintendent of Schools, said that ranch teachers *always* married cowboys, and that is why Wyoming has such an intelligent population.

Despite *The Virginian's* success, Wister never attempted a sequel. Some say that is because he once read his obituaries and was discouraged by the criticism in them. When his father-in-law died in 1910, some newspapers confused the dead man with Wister and printed obituaries calling him a "first rate, second-rate author."

Even Wister's mother, a Philadelphian who wore white kid gloves at dinner parties even while she carved, criticized her son's writing. She complained that *The Virginian* was piecemeal, the last chapter superfluous, and the heroine a failure. Wister agreed with his mother's opinion of Molly Wood; he admitted she was "without personality."

But Wister knew he had succeeded in creating the Virginian's character. "Never again can I light on a character so engaging. That only happens once even to the great ones of the earth."

Close-Up: DAVID ROBERTS

SEEMS AS IF EVERYBODY in Wyoming knows David Roberts. People never just say they *know* him, though; it's always "David's a good friend of mine," followed by an account of how he helped somebody out or gave someone a chance to get published or how he wrote something crazy in one of his columns.

David was already a respected journalist when I first met him in 1984. Nearly every year he won awards from the Wyoming State Press Association. He had even made national news in 1982, when he took a two-week leave of absence from the weekly paper he founded, the *Medicine Bow Post*, and joined the staff of the *Post* in Washington D. C.

In a story he wrote for the *Washington Post* about that exchange, he described himself as "someone who is skinny and who wears excess clothing that would make most people unbearably hot." Sure enough, on the warm summer day when we first met, he was wearing a sweater. His dark brown hair, long in front, fell over his forehead as he talked.

Sitting at the picnic table outside the old Union Pacific depot in Medicine Bow, his Pentax camera hanging from his neck, Roberts talked about his native state, which he once defined as "a cowboy riding his horse all the way to town to find everything closed."

"Wyoming's a liberal state," he said "in that people expect you to have strong opinions. They'll probably disagree with you, but they'll grant you the right to say what you think."

Everything about him spelled "genial," from his soft drawl to the smile that spread across his face. But David Roberts held strong opinions. What other newspaper publisher would write editorials advocating gun control in the heart of cowboy country? Who else would express doubts about the safety of nuclear energy, knowing that some of his subscribers worked at a nearby uranium mine?

"I got a few letters on that one. Jobs are important to people. But the only time I really got into trouble was when I started a campaign to pave the streets."

He chuckled, then tried to explain his critics' rationale. "When you get too close, hit people where they're most vulnerable—in their pocketbooks—you get into trouble. I think a lot of folks were afraid that the boom would end, people would be leaving town, and whoever was left would get stuck with unbearable taxes. And I suppose you could say they were right, with all the lay-offs at the coal and uranium mines. The energy boom ended a whole lot sooner than I ever thought it would."

Still, he couldn't resist goading his readers with cartoons about the street situation—and with slogans. STOMP OUT MUD!

David estimated that the *Post* had 1,000 subscribers then. Not bad, in a town where the population had dwindled from about 950 to 750 over the past three years. He had a wall map in his office with red-tipped pins showing where his subscribers lived. "We don't have anyone in Hawaii or in Maine. Other than that, we're in just about every state in the Union."

"We try to include a little something for everyone. Some people like the recipes. Some turn first thing to the police report, for laughs." David's all-time favorite was the Drunken Dog report. He broke up laughing telling about it. It seems a Medicine Bow citizen called the police to complain that a man outside the Virginian Hotel was trying to get a dog drunk, that he was pouring beer down the dog's throat. When the police investigated, they learned that the dog had drunk anti-freeze and that the liquid in the beer bottle was actually salt water, which the man was giving the dog to induce vomiting. "Thank goodness there was a logical explanation!" David said.

David Roberts made a name for the Medicine Bow Post *and made a barter with the* Washington Post.

The Opinion Page was the section of the paper David had the most fun with and the part that brought him the most awards and subscribers. "Phyllis Optical" was a collection of poems he composed late at night, just before deadline. "Post Age" was his commentary on events of the week. "A Story to Forget" evolved from his attempt to read *Moral Discourses* by Epictetus during a long, snowbound winter. As for his editorials—a visiting reporter accused him of stirring up controversy at town council meetings just so he would have something to write.

In January 1982, when temperatures in Medicine Bow were approaching thirty-five below zero and nobody was venturing outside any more than necessary, David wrote to Katherine Graham, publisher of the *Washington Post*. "Hello from Medicine Bow, Wyoming, the heart of the American West. Like Washington D.C., the town of Medicine Bow has a *Post* too." He told Graham he was a long-time admirer of her newspaper, and that was one reason he named his paper the *Post*. Then he asked, would she be interested in exchanging reporters for a couple of weeks?

He said later that he wanted to show that "community journalism, even at its smallest, is an exciting field where anything can happen."

In April he received a reply. "The editors here are intrigued and would like to take you up on your proposal." David spent the last two weeks of June that year at the *Washington Post*, while reporter Chip Brown took over the Medicine Bow newspaper. It was David's first time east of Bassett, Nebraska.

He had a wonderful time, he said, observing newspaper operations, meeting staff, and attending editorial conferences and a White House press briefing. His only disappointment was that he wasn't allowed to do more writing. "There were several stories I wanted to do from a Wyoming viewpoint, but the Newspaper Guild wouldn't allow it. They'd only let me do stories their reporters couldn't cover."

Although staff members welcomed him, David said he felt a little conspicuous in Washington D.C. "I kept walking around with my camera hanging around my neck. Back there, reporters don't take pictures, photographers don't write, and feature writers get two whole weeks to write one excellent story. I would just love that!" Meanwhile, in Medicine Bow, Chip Brown, who was used to writing one excellent story every two weeks, struggled to produce enough copy—and photos—to fill Medicine Bow's paper.

In the article Roberts wrote for the front page of the *Washington Post*, he contrasted Washington D.C. with Medicine Bow, Wyoming.

Washington D.C. has paved streets. Medicine Bow has dirt streets. The D.C. telephone directory has too many pages to count; the Medicine Bow telephone book has basically four pages. Medicine Bow has about 953 people, 117 dogs and 76 cats; Washington D.C. has more.

He went on to comment about D.C. street crime, fear in subways, poverty, and the responsibility of politicians in this "showcase city of the world."

I can't imagine a politician's going to work in the capital city and not feeling an obligation to help the people who are in serious economic need. Back home, people seem to help one another because there is no pride in having a community with ill or needy or troubled residents. No one is isolated from problems in a small town and therefore, perhaps, everyone seems to assist in seeking solutions.

A highlight of his stay in Washington was a meeting with Katherine Graham. He was still in touch with her when we talked, and had sent her some chocolate-covered huckleberries that Christmas.

A freight train rolled by, making conversation impossible. Roberts responded with his classic slow smile.

"Train break. Around here, instead of coffee breaks, we take train breaks. They come through four times an hour. One time last year AMTRAK actually stopped at Medicine Bow, did you hear about that? I was sitting right here when it happened—had my camera with me—got a whole front-page story."

An elderly passenger from Chicago had become upset with the train attendant sitting across from her because he kept jangling the change in his pocket. She asked him to stop, but he went right on jangling his change. Finally the noise made her so nervous, she told him if he didn't quit, she'd shoot him in the leg. That's when they stopped the train. "They booked her right here in the city jail. Poor old lady had to wait for relatives to come bail her out. She really did have a revolver in her bag."

He thought about the pathos in her story. "Sometimes you can't be funny. Sometimes, after writing all day and going to meetings every night of the week, you're too tired to go home and write something humorous. And there are times when tragedy comes. When something bad happens to just one family, it affects everybody in town. It affects the newspaper."

But being gloomy all the time wouldn't do either. "I could write an editorial every week about how many folks are losing their jobs. But that wouldn't help anybody."

Wyoming needs better transportation and a more diversified economy if it is ever going to escape the boom-bust cycle, David said. "If we base our economy on just mining and ranching, we'll never get our streets paved. But it's hard, when we're so isolated."

He said that at Riverton, Wyoming, a town of about 10,000, a few people had started a business manufacturing compasses. "It's just a small operation, but that's the kind of development we need here. Our Chamber of Commerce is working on it." Roberts was president of the Chamber that year.

When Roberts started the *Post* he didn't expect to make much money for the first three years. But the way things turned out, he was making even less money seven years after he'd founded the paper. He'd started out paying himself a 500-dollar-a-month salary when the money was there. But now the money was hardly ever there, and he said he'd rather pay his bills than take a salary; he couldn't stomach the thought of going into debt. "I'd like to think that when I leave, this town will be a little better off than when I came."

I asked him whether he thought very often about leaving Medicine Bow.

"Allllllllll the time," he drawled. "But I'd have to know I was leaving the paper in good hands. The trouble is, I'm not sure anybody else would put up with this—the broken-down equipment, long hours, no money, the meetings. If people have a meeting they go to once a week, they expect me to be there every time. It doesn't matter that I have to show up at meetings every single night and they only go to one a week. What they really want is for my camera to come. I just happen to have the neck that the camera hangs around most of the time."

Town council meetings were the worst. At Thanksgiving he wrote that he had "more things to be thankful for than the city council has closed executive sessions." In another column he speculated that "hell is having to attend a city council meeting that never ends," and wished for a "rust-proof robot" to attend council meetings in his place.

Still, he said, in some ways he enjoyed running his own newspaper. He liked being his own boss, setting his own hours. "Some awfully interesting people come through here in the summers—bicyclists, walkers for various causes, a procession of antique cars—I do get to meet a lot of people. And it's nice, walking through town and knowing just about everybody. These are good people. There isn't anybody here I hate, or even dislike. There are some I disagree with, though.

"The main thing is when I came here, I told myself five years was as long as anybody should stay at one newspaper. I'm in my eighth year now, and I'm afraid I'm beginning to mellow. Yes, I am definitely mellowing out."

We walked across the street to the Virginian Hotel and ordered dinner, a noontime meal. People in the coffee shop kept stopping at our table to talk with David: the president of the National Woolgrowers Association, the superintendent of schools, and a middle-aged woman in jeans and a t-shirt.

"Hello, David," the woman said. "I saw your Nova across the street and came in to see how you're doing."

"Well hello, Gladys. How are you getting along? Do you have any news for me?"

"After this weekend I will. Rowdy and Verna are getting married, and our whole family's driving up to Lovell for the wedding."

"Is that right? I'll have to check back with you on that. I'll be sure to call you the first of next week."

The woman left, and David took up a spoonful of cold soup. "Did I tell you I wrote to the *Jerusalem Post?* They said I'll have to learn Hebrew before we can work out any kind of exchange. I don't know if I can do that and still get time to run the newspaper."

He smiled, giving the impression that he just might try.

جر

David donated the *Medicine Bow Post* to the University of Wyoming journalism department in 1989. UW journalism majors now publish the weekly paper. He taught journalism at the University of Wyoming and then entered the graduate school of journalism at the University of Nebraska.

Chapter 9

Rawlins

RAWLINS, Wyoming's ninth largest town
Population 9,380   *Elevation 6,755*
*Question: What contribution did Rawlins make to the Brooklyn Bridge?

Places to Visit

•• Information Center in Union Pacific caboose, next to Rip Griffin Truck Stop, I-80 and Higley Boulevard.
•• Wyoming Frontier Prison, Walnut at Fifth Street. Tours $3.00; less for children and senior citizens.
•• Carbon County Museum, Walnut at Ninth Street. Free.
•• Ferris Mansion, 607 W. Maple Street, a bed and breakfast inn where copper mine owner George Ferris once lived. Tours for a small fee.
•• Washington Park, near Walnut and Fourteenth streets, for picnicking and relaxation.
•• Town mural on building at Cedar and Third streets.

A Brief Background

From the Interstate, during the summer Rawlins can seem all desert heat and highway construction. But drive into town and you will discover Victorian houses on tree-lined streets, spacious parks, and small-town friendliness.

The Ferris Mansion, now a bed-and-breakfast, was once the home of George Ferris, a copper mine owner.

Rawlins was named for a U.S. Army Chief of Staff who helped survey the route for the Union Pacific Railroad in 1867. He drank from a spring here, called it the most refreshing drink he had ever tasted, and declared, "If anything is ever named after me, I hope it will be a spring of water."

Rawlins is county seat of Carbon County, an area rich in low-sulfur coal, natural gas, oil, and uranium. Most of the earliest buildings in town are native sandstone.

Two hematite (iron oxide) mines near town supplied Rawlins Red paint for Union Pacific Railroad cars. The railroad owned the mines until 1878.

Thomas Edison visited Rawlins with a group of scientists in 1878 to view the solar eclipse. The group went fishing afterwards at Battle Lake, southeast of Rawlins, and here, some people claim, Edison found inspiration to work out the

The Frontier Prison, used from 1901 to 1981, is the main tourist attraction in Rawlins.

details of his incandescent lamp. Butch Cassidy and his Wild Bunch lived for awhile near Battle Lake.

Calamity Jane was a frequent Rawlins visitor. Buffalo Bill Cody once worked as a U.S. Army guide out of Fort Fred Steele.

Wyoming's state penitentiary is at Rawlins. The Frontier Prison, used from 1901 to 1981, is the main tourist attraction, and its grounds are often used for community festivities. If you like stories of outlaws and lynchings and have always wanted to see a "do-it-yourself" gallows, take the prison tour. Just don't confuse frontier practices with Wyoming's penal system today. (See Close-Up.)

Rawlins's most macabre story is of Big Nose George Parrott, a convicted robber who, with his partner, Dutch Charlie, killed two men in a prison escape attempt. Townspeople lynched them in 1880, where the Union Pacific depot now stands. (The Town of Medicine Bow re-enacts the hanging of Dutch Charlie each summer.)

After the hanging, three Rawlins physicians—Union Pacific Doctor Thomas McGee, first woman doctor west of the Mississippi, Lillian Heath, and John Osborne, who was later elected Governor of Wyoming—removed the top of Big Nose George's skull so they could study his brain and learn whether its structure differed from that of law-abiding citizens.

Dr. Heath later donated the skull cap to the Union Pacific Railroad Museum in Omaha. The remainder of the skull was discovered by construction workers in 1950, in a whiskey barrel behind Dr. McGee's former office. It is on display now at the county museum.

Dr. Osborne had a lampshade, a death mask, and shoes made from Big Nose George's skin. You can see the shoes—and many other artifacts of the Old West—at the Carbon County Museum.

⨎

*Answer: The Brooklyn Bridge's first coat of paint was Rawlins Red, from nearby hematite mines.

About the Close-Ups

•• Nobody knows Rawlins's history as well as Rans Baker. It's varied, it's funny, and it's macabre. Let him tell you.

•• Bill Carlisle was a likable bandit who wouldn't steal from women and children and who took pains never to physically harm anybody. Read about this "Robin Hood of the Rails."

•• Abe De Herrera helped transform Rawlins's police department as the community grew and changed. The story this former police chief tells might be duplicated in many small towns. But De Herrera is not an ordinary man.

•• Wyoming's State Penitentiary is nothing like the one of

Nobody knows Rawlins history like Rans Baker. It's varied, it's funny, and it's macabre.

frontier times. Warden Duane Shillinger tells us how he runs the penitentiary today. Some say he is fifty years ahead of his time.

Close-Up: RANS BAKER

RANS BAKER LIVES WITH HIS wife on a quiet Rawlins street with few distractions—except for the squirrels. "Go away! I haven't got time to play with you!" he tells one climbing his screen door. He opens the door and feeds the squirrel a peanut.

"In the winter it's the deer. We had such a hard winter in 1984. Game and Fish brought the wounded deer to the old penitentiary grounds. We had this unspoken agreement that some of us would take care of them. Our little herd averages twenty-two to twenty-eight does and fawns now. They drift in and out all year round.

"In the fall of the year it's wonderful, going up to the park and to the old 'pen' and watching the bucks trying their horns. Game and Fish isn't thrilled about our feeding them apples, but the deer know where every apple tree in town is, anyway. Apples aren't really nutritious for them, but they like them. They're like candy. I always slice them so the little ones can get some too. I have a couple of bruises on my shins—those does get tired of waiting, and they can kick pretty hard.

"There's a lot of beauty to this country if you know where to look. We have all manner of birds, high desert varieties. We have a beautiful selection of migrating songbirds. It's a fragile beauty. We have wildflowers that may lie dormant for five or six years, then we have a wet year and they're in bloom."

Baker is almost a Rawlins native. He moved here from McFadden as a small boy. "My adoptive father was a doctor. He had to *buy* a medical practice in order for us to move here. Now they pay doctors to come. You can find McFadden listed in *Ghost Towns of Wyoming* now. It's an eerie thing to outlive your town."

History is Baker's passion—history and sculpture. In the Rawlins library, at Third and Buffalo streets, you can see his dioramas of Carbon County history. Everything is historically accurate, built to one-thirty-second scale, just like the toy soldiers he played with as a boy. And like those soldiers, his figures are made of lead. One of his favorites is a frontier saloon scene which Baker titled "Rawlins Parks and Recreation Department."

Baker does research for the library and gives lectures on Carbon County history. He said Rawlins is much more than a railroad and prison town. "Rawlins had good water in the middle of the desert. That's the important thing."

In the early days Rawlins was an Indian battleground. The Utes, Shoshones, Crows, Sioux, and Arapahos all frequented the area, but none of them ever lived here year-round. "Rawlins was right in the middle of No-Man's Land," Baker said.

Two military forts played a part in Rawlins history: Fort Fred Steele, six miles east of town, and Fort Halleck, at the northwest corner of Elk Mountain. Fort Steele was built to protect the railroad, and Fort Halleck provided protection to the Pony Express. "There wasn't a day at Fort Halleck that wasn't an adventure," Baker said. "It's the sort of things 'B' movies are made out of. Sometimes they'd get down to just three shells per man. They'd have to lock themselves in at night and let the animals and the Indians have the parade grounds, and then reclaim them in the morning. It wasn't a problem, because there wasn't anything there that the Indians wanted anyway."

Rawlins became a major shipping town, forwarding supplies to the Indian reservations and to military posts, Baker said. It was also a major shipping point for cattle. "We had big stockyards here. Medicine Bow was the only nearby town of any size. When Rawlins was given the county seat, the political power wound up here."

Rawlins had its gold rushes too. "The early one was a big hoax—it lasted a week," Baker said. Gold was discovered in Rawlins Red paint, in the hematite mines. It all had to do with mineral rights law. Paint and iron aren't precious metals, but gold is. Anyone who discovered a precious metal on someone else's property could lay claim to it. The two paint companies exchanged ownerships during that week, each laying claim to the other's gold.

"The town was surrounded by a forest of claim stakes. But people were laughing at themselves, and nobody got mad about it. Rawlins has a wonderful sense of humor. It's perverted—but it's humor."

A later silver and gold rush at Seminoe, north of Rawlins, ended when Sioux and Arapaho Indians attacked the miners. If gold prices rise sharply, that area may be mined again.

Cattle ranches flourished during the 1880s, but by the end of the decade Rawlins was center for the Wyoming sheep industry. "We had major flockmeisters," said Baker. "Wool remained big in Carbon County until after World War II."

Several of the Victorian mansions in town were built by sheep ranchers. Maple Street was sometimes known as Sheepman's Row, but more often it was called Capital Hill. "Capital as in dollars."

Bill Carlisle wasn't the first train robber who wouldn't steal from women or children, Baker said. In 1878 four men staged a hold-up. They walked from Cheyenne to Medicine Bow—more than one hundred miles—built a river raft, sailed down the Medicine Bow River to the Platte River, then walked toward Percy, their targeted station near Rawlins, but got lost and stumbled on to the wrong stop. When they finally found Percy, they put on white masks, boarded a Pullman car, robbed only the men on board, and traipsed off into the night with a take of 250 dollars, two watches with matching chains, a railroad pass and a conductor's key. A posse riding the finest Rawlins horses searched for the robbers several days before finally capturing them.

Big Nose George Parrott and his partner, Dutch Charlie, staged a robbery soon afterwards, in which they derailed the train. Later, townspeople killed them by lynching, but lynching didn't always result in death, Baker said. Sometimes an offender was choked, as a warning, then set free.

Cutting off Big Nose George's skull cap wasn't unique in those times, Baker said. It provided an opportunity to study a criminal's brain. "This was exactly the same thing they did after the assassination of President Garfield. The Smithsonian still has his assassin's brain. The extra step—tanning the man's hide—Rawlins wasn't the first with that either. The same thing happened to a child molester north of Rawlins earlier on.

"They turned Big Nose George into a pair of shoes. Our first Democratic governor wore them when he was inaugurated—Governor John Osborne. They're a little worn now, but they're at the museum. You can still see them."

✎

Another scratch on the door. "No, go away! I know it's eleven o'clock, but I can't play with you now."

Baker carries a bag of nuts into the front yard, puts some into a feeder and gives the rest to a dozen charging squirrels. "I have to buy almonds, walnuts and peanuts in 50-pound bags. But that's all right, I eat them too."

Close-Up: BILL CARLISLE
WANTED DEAD OR ALIVE—BILL CARLISLE
$5600 REWARD

ALL ALONG THE UNION Pacific Railroad line in 1916, from Omaha to Salt Lake City, posters urged the capture of a gentle bandit who wouldn't steal from women and who took pains never to physically harm anyone. Legend held that he committed one of his robberies with a child's toy glass gun.

Known as "The Lone Bandit," "The Man in the White Mask" (he wore a white handkerchief), and "Robin Hood of the Rails," Bill Carlisle was the last of the robbers who held up the Union Pacific during the first two decades of this century.

He committed his first train robbery at Green River, Wyoming, near midnight on February 9, 1916. The twenty-five-year-old drifter had come there in search of a job on the railroad. The railroad wasn't hiring.

"I was desperate," Carlisle later recalled. "Hungry, cold, jobless, with only a nickel in my pocket.... While I was standing at the station waiting to jump a freight, the Overland Limited came through. I stood looking at the warm, comfortable coaches with their bright lights and well-dressed people.... The idea of holding up the train came to me on the spur of the moment. That train pulled out, but while I was still wondering what to do, another passenger train pulled in and I got on."

He entered a Pullman car, pulled out his gun, and ordered the terrified porter to collect money and valuables from all the adult male passengers. "Don't open any berths occupied by women and children," Carlisle told him. Neither did he take money from the porter. "You'll get few tips this trip," he sympathized. That first hold-up netted Carlisle $52.35.

Union Pacific officials called the robbery "fool's luck" and posted a $1500 reward for Carlisle's capture. It was practically unheard of for a lone bandit to hold up a train. "It could never happen again," the officials declared.

But on April 5 Carlisle robbed the Overland Limited a few miles west of Cheyenne. This time the porter's collection totalled $506.07. A few frightened women put money into the hat, but Carlisle gave it back to them. The Union Pacific increased the bounty on Carlisle's head to $5600.

Feeling obliged to take action, law officials arrested several known criminals who had no alibis for the nights of February 9 and April 5. When Carlisle learned of the arrests, he wrote a letter to the *Denver Post* announcing that he was the bandit, and to prove it, he enclosed a gold watch chain taken during the second hold-up. To convince the public further, he promised, "I will hold up the next Union Pacific train west of Laramie."

Authorities insisted the outlaw was merely trying to create a diversion, but two weeks later, true to his word, Carlisle robbed the male passengers of $378.50 on a train near Hanna, west of Laramie. To be sure he received credit for his earlier accomplishments, Carlisle showed his victims the watch which matched the chain he had mailed to the *Denver Post* earlier.

Carlisle's success was short-lived. As the train rounded a curve, Carlisle jumped off, severely twisting his ankle. Barely able to walk, he hid in some bushes along the North Platte River until a posse found him early in the morning.

Carlisle spotted the men before they saw him, and he could easily have shot several of them. But he chose not to. The next day's *Denver Post* carried the headline, "Bandit Surrenders Rather Than Turn Killer — Lays Down His Guns When Officers Are Afraid to Disarm Him."

Carlisle received a life sentence to the Wyoming State Penitentiary at Rawlins, but after he had spent three years there, his sentence was reduced to fifty years. Perhaps he should have felt grateful. Instead, he staged an elaborate escape.

He had a packing crate built in the prison shirt factory, climbed inside it, and had himself delivered to the local freight office. Two weeks later he robbed another Wyoming train, just outside Medicine Bow.

But then his luck ran out. He hadn't realized the coach would be filled with soldiers returning from World War I. He passed his hat to the few civilians on board and told the doughboys, "Keep your money, boys. I don't want it." A guard jumped him as he leaped off the train, and Carlisle's gun went off, wounding Carlisle in the hand and wrist.

Carlisle eluded the law for the next ten days. Ranchers and homesteaders sympathized with the soft-spoken felon. They provided him food and shelter, bandaged his wounds, and even invited him to a community dance. When lawmen finally cornered him, Carlisle surrendered peacefully, not wanting to endanger his hosts. He was critically wounded during his capture.

The sheriff ordered Carlisle to raise his hands, even though Carlisle was unarmed. He complied, but then because of the sharp pain in his injured wrist, he lowered one arm, and the sheriff shot Carlisle in the lung. Carlisle nearly died, but after several months he was well enough to return to prison.

At the penitentiary he enrolled in a correspondence course in business, learned to type, and became the prison librarian. By the time he was eligible for parole in 1936, he had so impressed the prison chaplain that the chaplain told prison officials, "Should Bill Carlisle ever commit another crime, I will serve time either for him or with him."

Carlisle was flooded with marriage proposals just before his release, and a Hollywood film studio asked him to star in a movie about his life. The chaplain advised him to refuse the offer.

He didn't disappoint the chaplain. After his release Carlisle married a registered nurse, adopted a child, and became a successful businessman in Laramie, opening a motor court and drive-in restaurant where Aspen Square is now. A Laramie resident who once worked as a carhop for Carlisle described him as "a nice old man who never spoke a cross word to anybody."

After his reform Carlisle often gave lectures on crime, and even appeared on two national radio shows, *Calling All Cars* and *Crime Doesn't Pay*. He published his autobiography in 1946, with illustrations by Charlie Russell. The Governor of Wyoming granted him a full pardon the following year.

During the fifties, in an article in the *Laramie Boomerang*, a reporter called Carlisle "an outstanding citizen" and touted his bowling average—one hundred sixty-five. Carlisle died in 1965, at age seventy-four.

Carlisle paid for his brief criminal career with a critical injury and nineteen years in prison, more than most murderers serve. But his flamboyance brought him the attention he craved, and his non-violence earned him affection from a public who appreciated a bandit with principles. "I never shot a man or took money from a woman or child," said Bill Carlisle.

Close-Up: ABE DE HERRERA

ABE DE HERRERA GREW UP at a railroad section camp between Rawlins and Wamsutter, as one of eight children. His is the fourth generation of his family to live in Wyoming. His ancestors were sheepherders.

Because the school at the section camp went only through the eighth grade, Abe and his brother moved together to Rawlins to attend high school. They bussed dishes at a restaurant to pay their living expenses.

The brothers took up amateur boxing, and both were promised scholarships to Idaho State University. But when boxing was discontinued as a college sport, the scholarships were cancelled. Abe's brother enlisted in the army.

Abe De Herrera got married, started raising a family, and continued working at the restaurant. "The only jobs they hired Spanish-speaking people for were labor jobs. I saw how my dad worked, as a laborer on the railroad. I didn't want any part of that," De Herrera said.

De Herrera and his wife tried to rent a small apartment uptown. "It wasn't fancy at all. When I went up to look at it, the owner took the 'For Rent' sign down. We made our home on the south side of Rawlins then, the Hispanic section."

In 1965 De Herrera's boxing coach told him the Rawlins Police Department was accepting applications for employment. He applied, took a test that "didn't even relate to police

Former police chief Abe De Herrera helped transform Rawlins's police department.

work," and scored third highest. He was hired that summer, when he was twenty-two.

"I was thrilled. I expected to go to school, to get training, but I was on the police force four years before I had any formal training. I had to furnish my own uniform; I had to furnish my own weapon. I had no idea how to handle that weapon I was carrying. I relied on the officer I was working with to train me.

"That's the way police departments handled their people then. One day you were a private citizen, the next day you were a patrolman. If I heard of a class in Casper put on by the Highway Patrol, I would catch a ride with a highway patrolman and go on my own time. Or a lot of times I'd go to a class at the penitentiary."

After four years as a patrolman De Herrera was promoted to sergeant. "Rawlins was in the last stages of the Old West then, where there was gambling and prostitution. It had been common practice to escort the prostitutes to city hall and have them pay their weekly fine. I was involved when the department put an end to those illegal activities.

"The community began to grow; new businesses came to town. The old businesses on skid row started moving out. Housing developments came in, with the coal mines opening in Hanna. We absorbed some growth in Rawlins from people who couldn't find a place to live in Rock Springs during the boom years.

"I was promoted to lieutenant of the patrol division, and I saw myself not at the bottom of the pole anymore. During the seventies we had a police chief who came in from Indiana, and he made me assistant chief of police. When he left, in 1977, I was promoted to chief.

"I saw the department change where the court was no longer a part of the police department. Up until then a police officer served as court bailiff. I couldn't see ourselves being together.

"I convinced the mayor and city council to help me put in place certain provisions regarding the recruiting and screening of police officers. We incorporated mandatory training. We completely changed the image of the police department.

"I told the city council, 'The jail is outdated, it needs to be closed down. It's not fit for dogs.' I wanted to send prisoners to the county jail, but the sheriff didn't want them. At the city jail we had no one to watch prisoners at night.

"The whole thing came to a crash when a young man came in and was arrested at the hospital for a misdemeanor. He never should have been in our jail. The hospital didn't want him because he was rude. He committed suicide during the night in our jail. That led to a lawsuit—it woke up the community.

"There were other incidents where prisoners weren't treated right. Immigration would come in and ask for our help to round up illegal aliens. They would round them up like sheep—mostly Mexicans. I went in one morning and there must have been forty of them, jammed into three cells. I had to inform Immigration that that wasn't going to happen any more, not while I was there.

"I went through two or three lawsuits where I had to answer for what I did. In my depositions in those lawsuits I wouldn't conceal the truth behind these problems. I was honest—I laid things on the line. This led me into trouble.

"One night our officers locked up a man with a head injury, bleeding and drunk, and failed to monitor him. The next morning we had a dead man in our jail, and I had to answer for it. I took affidavits from the officers on duty. We were grossly negligent. I refused to throw those affidavits away.

"By admitting that we were wrong, I made enemies. A certain faction of officers considered me a traitor. Rumors started circulating in the community that I let Mexicans loose, that I was selling drugs. I honestly believe the city manager thought these rumors were true. He called for an inquiry, and he told me he was going to replace me with a more professional individual with a college education.

"I asked the city manager for specific reasons for my dismissal so I could face my accusers and clear my name. He wouldn't give me any, so I refused to resign. He fired me in November, 1981, and appointed as police chief an officer with less training than I had. I asked the city council for a hearing then, but my request was denied.

"The summer of 1981 I had an accident down at the police department. Someone had spilled silicone boot spray on the floor, and I slipped on it and hurt my back. Later doctors realized that I had a broken vertebra."

De Herrera went through several painful back surgeries. He was declared thirty per cent disabled but he wasn't ready to retire. He applied to go back to work as a police officer, doing clerical work, but the new chief refused to hire him. "I pleaded with the police chief, I pleaded with the city council, I pleaded with the city manager, and their response was to get rid of me."

Years earlier De Herrera's brother had been discharged from the army with a one hundred per cent disability. He had enrolled at the University of Wyoming then and had become the first Hispanic to graduate from the University of Wyoming law school. He helped Abe file suit to gain back pay and benefits and a full retirement pension.

De Herrera said that the people who had called for his firing were new to Rawlins and didn't know his reputation for integrity. Long-time residents continued to support him, he said, and in 1986 De Herrera was elected to the Rawlins City Council. During his first year in office, he persuaded the council to close the city jail. City offenders are now either released on bail or on their own recognizance or are booked through the county system.

A few years ago De Herrera enrolled at the University of Wyoming to study elementary education, with concentrations in Spanish and middle school. "Going after a higher education was a goal that had been there all the time," he said. "I served eighteen years on the school board in Rawlins. I'd gotten involved at Head Start. My wife and I were involved with PTA. We thought it was our responsibility, as parents."

He described his first semester at the University as "frightening."

"I was afraid I was going to be the only old guy up here; afraid of the intelligence that is associated with university campuses; afraid of not knowing how to write. I had been out of high school for twenty-eight years.

"Also, I could hardly walk. I had just gotten out of a full body cast and had just gotten a lower spine cast. I couldn't get to my classes on time. I had to meet with my professors and ask for help.

"But going back to school was something that I knew if I didn't do it now, I'd regret it the rest of my life. And it's paid off. I'm a good student.

"I'd like to go back to Pershing School, on my side of town, where a lot of teachers don't want to teach," De Herrera said. "To my knowledge Rawlins has never hired a Hispanic teacher, even though twenty per cent of the population is Hispanic."

His back injury continues to be a problem, and twice he suffered serious falls on campus. He won't let those stop him. "There're just too many good people in Rawlins who believe in me to just lie down."

His wife, who works for the Department of Family Services, has transferred from Rawlins to Laramie. One of their five daughters has enrolled at the university, and she and De Herrera are taking a class together. "I encouraged her to go back to school. I told her college isn't just for rich kids anymore. There is financial aid available."

De Herrera and his wife still own their home on Rawlins's south side. "Every time I go back to Rawlins, it reinforces my decision of coming to school," he said. "Right now the railroad is considering transferring still more people to jobs in other towns. Rawlins is a community that's lived with threats like that ever since I've lived there.

"Most of the coal mines in Hanna have closed. The uranium plant between Rawlins and Jeffrey City has closed. It used to employ two hundred eighty people, and most of those people lived in Rawlins. School enrollment is down; budgets are tight. I'd like to go back to Rawlins—it's my home—but I don't know if there'll be an opening there. I'd like to stay in Wyoming."

Close-Up: WARDEN DUANE SHILLINGER

A FEW YEARS AGO A Wyoming State Penitentiary inmate interviewed for a newspaper article described Duane Shillinger as "fifty years ahead of anyone else in America." Shillinger said the compliment probably referred to his "deprisonizing" Wyoming's state penitentiary.

"We try to upgrade the dignity of the offender—to bring him into a role of decision-making, a role of responsibility, a role of accountability. We try to enable the resident to realize that he has a stake in his destiny, that he is not just here to be warehoused.

"Each individual who enters here comes into my office, and he gets to know me and I get to know him. I spend time in their living areas, in their 'house,' as they call it. I have several men who are teaching me to play the guitar. I look forward to meeting with them—to going in and seeing them.

"They refer to me as 'Dad.' Like any parent, I want them to do their best. I screech at them. I expect things of them. As they put it, I'm 'on their case.'

"I have an affinity with these fellows. I don't sympathize with them; I just feel a concern. Many of them are lazy; many of them are angry; many of them have disputes they're carrying out, and they're wasting their time. I feel I can be effective in turning that around.

"I try to pump that same type of interest into my employees. We have a good staff here who promote wellness, who promote dignity, who promote a lifestyle without substance dependency."

The Rawlins penitentiary averages 733 inmates, with an additional 150 assigned to an honor farm at Riverton, 120 to a conservation camp at Newcastle, and 20 to a ninety-day military-style boot camp at Newcastle for young, first-time offenders. The women's prison, at Lusk, is separate.

Some say Wyoming State Penitentiary Warden Duane Shillinger is fifty years ahead of his time.

Eighty to ninety per cent of the inmates committed their crimes while under the influence of a substance, Shillinger said. Nearly thirty-five per cent of inmates who are transferred to honor facilities return to the Rawlins penitentiary because of substance violations.

"That's bothersome to me," said Shillinger. For the past two years he has been researching substance abuse by offenders. He had developed a treatment program—a "therapeutic community approach"—which began in 1992.

About half of those released on parole from the Rawlins penitentiary return to prison. Wyoming's community mental health workers, addiction support groups and business people offer support, Shillinger said, but most parolees don't stay in Wyoming, they return to their home states. Sixty per cent of the Rawlins inmates lived in Wyoming less than a year before they committed their crimes. A high percentage had been in Wyoming just two or three weeks.

Nearly half of the offenders have come to the penitentiary after lifetimes in foster homes, on probation, and in jail.

"I wouldn't want to go to jail. It would scare the dickens out of me," said Shillinger. "But it's part of their lifestyle. After they've been sleeping in alleys or under bridges or in the back ends of burned-out cars, drinking cheap wine, maybe going into 'DTs,' jail can be their rescue. They can get well, dry out, get their teeth fixed. That's their time to get healed."

Shillinger doesn't think prisons deter crime. "We need to work on prevention in the community. We need to strengthen the family, to do more in school systems, to provide more community support.

"Our schools have a tendency to deal with only those students who are easy to deal with. The problem student has been kicked out. That's the attitude out there in our society— if they can't fit in, kick them out. I get all these people who have been kicked out!

"The offender is not a popular person. Nobody likes to become a victim of a crime. I don't like criminal behavior, but I try to separate the behavior from the individual. The public is starting to realize that he is still a human, he is part of our group. We can't just kick people out."

In Indiana, legislators estimate the number of prison cells they will need by studying the behavior of second graders, Shillinger said. "That's frightening."

"The public pays dearly to maintain the incarcerated offender. They're also paying for behavior modification, where they can get a better product back. When they kick a guy out of the community, nine out of every ten inmates is going to be released back into that community within four or five years.

"The public feels to some extent that we're too lenient. Others are grateful that we're trying to restore a level of functionality. We receive a product from the community with a stamp of rejection. We take the failure-oriented and do what we can, working with the individual—it's a two-way street, of course—to bring his behavior up to a level where he is much more self-sufficient, where he feels more dignity and self-worth, where he has coping skills, social skills."

The inmates work, earning from five cents to fifty cents an hour, and they have to save their money if they want cable television or a stereo or want to take college courses. A wide range of vocational and academic courses is available. Men who are illiterate are required to take classes.

"We have some cardinal rules: Don't interrupt other students, and complete this amount of work in this period of time. If they want to take a break, they can."

Prisoners are allowed private visits with immediate family members. This practice is common in other countries, Shillinger said, but not in the United States.

"I've studied the Australian system, the Japanese system, and our neighbors to the south in Mexico. They're not embarrassed by life—by relationships and needs. They're just there. But our society has a problem with that.

"We have deprisonized as much as we can," said Shillinger. "That deprisonization has resulted in an absence of gangs, an absence of violence, an absence of rape culture, an absence of hard-core narcotics. There are drugs that come in here. Now, with drugs that can be placed on a stamp and mailed into the institution, we have a problem. But thank God, we're basically limited to marijuana.

"Last Christmas we had four hundred fifty tabs of LSD concealed in a Christmas card. God knows what would have happened if that had gone through! We could have had people involved in violence, people overdosing. It was a potential tragedy.

"What we try to do is work on the idea of community. This is their community, and if they inject drugs, they're going to destroy a stable, respectful community.

"People often say there has to be a flaw in a person to stay in a place like this," Shillinger said. "I guess I have that particular flaw. I have lived and breathed penitentiary for twenty-five years.

"I have known poverty. I grew up on a Crow Indian reservation in Montana, in a house without electric lights and without plumbing. My dad had a small dry land farm. He took a railroad boxcar and converted it into a home, and we lived in that boxcar house for fourteen years.

"I understand poverty. I understand why people want to give up. I also understand why people shouldn't give up. I understand that education is the key—that education will move you out of muck and mire.

"That's why I tell the individuals here, 'You don't have to settle for this.'"

‡

Chapter 10

Rawlins to Rock Springs

*Question: What happened at Tipton, just west of Red Desert, in 1900?

A Brief Background

People complain about the 108-mile drive from Rawlins to Rock Springs. They say the landscape is desolate—there's nothing there. You, too, may find that you are driving too fast, cursing the monotony, and longing for trees, green lawns, houses, and people.

You might as well slow down and smell the sagebrush, all thirteen varieties. You can watch for antelope, too, and horses. Any groups of horses you see in unfenced areas here are probably wild.

You will cross the Continental Divide twice within the next seventy miles. If you look at a Wyoming map, you will see that north of Superior, the Continental Divide line separates into two branches, enclosing about forty-two hundred square miles in the Great Divide Basin, before coming together again south of Rawlins. No drainage reaches the ocean from this basin; moisture flows out into alkali flats and evaporates. The basin encompasses most of the Red Desert, which gets just six-and-a-half to seven inches of rainfall per year.

You won't find many stopping places between Rawlins and Rock Springs, but these are a few landmarks.

•• Red Rim, twelve miles west of Rawlins. The Wyoming Wildlife and National Wildlife Federations are building a visitors' center here dedicated to pronghorn antelope (The pronghorn is not a true antelope, but is the sole representative of another family.) Dense sagebrush makes this an ideal winter range for pronghorn, and not all ranchers are happy about that.

In 1983, Taylor Lawrence built an antelope-proof fence to keep a herd of twenty-four hundred pronghorn from moving onto his ranch. Wildlife advocates sued, and the U.S. Supreme Court ruled that Lawrence's fence must come down. Now another area rancher, Stan Jolley, is carrying out a five-year project on Wyoming Game and Fish Department land to show that livestock and wildlife can co-exist here.

•• Wamsutter (population 240). Wamsutter is the oldest continually occupied town within the Great Divide Basin. It started as a railroad section camp and was named for a German bridge builder on the Union Pacific. The Overland Trail ran fifteen miles south of here. Today most of Wamsutter's residents work at oil and gas wells or at a uranium mine.

•• Table Rock, a company town owned by Colorado Interstate Gas Company. Table Rock was also known as Pulpit Rock, because here in 1847 Brigham Young preached a sermon to Mormons on their way to Utah.

•• Point of Rocks, named for a sandstone ridge jutting out over Bitter Creek. South of here, in 1872, two prospectors "salted" the countryside with diamonds, rubies, garnets, sapphires, emeralds, and amethysts. They planted all the gems together, in anthills, and led potential investors to the site after blindfolding them and making them hike cross-country for four days.

Two California bankers paid the prospectors six hundred thousand dollars for the rights to the precious gem fields and floated a public stock issue of twelve million dollars. Even New York jeweler Charles Tiffany was taken in by the scam, calling the gems a "rajah's ransom."

Clarence King, who had been commissioned by the U.S. War Department to conduct a survey across the Fortieth Parallel, investigated, hoping to share in the riches, and discovered that the fields were a fraud. King announced his finding, the bankers repaid all the stockholders, and King became a hero for a short time. The prospectors never paid back the money. They were later murdered.

Point of Rocks has the remains of a stage station used during the 1860s on the Overland Trail. It also has the biggest electric power plant in Wyoming, eight miles north of town.

Three thousand construction workers built the Jim Bridger Power Plant from 1970 to 1974, working twelve hours a day, seven days a week. They lived in trailers or camped on the desert, and one man supposedly built his home out of tumbleweeds. The workers made good money, but about the only places they could go for recreation were the desert and the Point of Rocks bar.

People still tell stories about the heavy drinking and fighting that went on here. One of the strangest tales is of a man who shot and killed his girlfriend. Even though he confessed, he was never charged with murder, because nobody knew the woman's name or where she was from—or so people say.

Today workers commute from Rock Springs to the power plant and to Black Butte coal mine southeast of Point of Rocks.
•• Superior (population 273) is a recommended detour five miles north of the Interstate. Superior is a former coal mining town with Old West architecture and the largest union hall in Wyoming. Five thousand people lived here until Union

Superior, Wyoming, a former coal mining town with Old West architecture is a recommended detour.

Pacific switched from coal-fired engines to diesel fuel during the mid-1950s. Present-day residents are converting the union hall into a visitors' center, using funds from the Abandoned Land Mines reclamation program. In 1991 the opening scene of the feature movie *Leaving Normal* was filmed here.

When you entered Sweetwater County, just west of Rawlins, you entered the only Wyoming county to consistently vote Democratic, and the second-richest county in the state. (Only Campbell County, in northern Wyoming, is wealthier.) The county's wealth comes from taxes levied on coal, natural gas, oil, trona, uranium, and bentonite.

Although mining is the main source of income here, Sweetwater County also has ranchers. Most of the land in this area is owned or leased by the Rock Springs Grazing Association, which controls two million acres and leases more land from the Bureau of Land Management than anyone else in the United States.

Some people say they could devote a lifetime to exploring the Red Desert and still not get enough of it.

Although you can't appreciate it from the Interstate, the Red Desert is a rich and varied place—and it is an easy side trip from Rock Springs. If you follow Highway 191 ten miles north out of town, you will come to the Tri-Territory Loop road, which will take you into the desert. Better yet, stop at the Bureau of Land Management office on Highway 191 just north of town and pick up a detailed map of the area.

One of the Red Desert's main attractions is the Killpecker Sand Dunes. That's right, *Killpecker*, as in Killpecker Creek, named by disgruntled men who suffered the effects of drinking the creek's salty water.

The dunes are twenty thousand years old, and some say they are the largest "living" (moving) ones outside the Sahara Desert. They extend east fifty-five miles and range from two to ten miles wide. Constant winds cause the dunes to move and shift into new patterns, and because the dunes are continually moving, vegetation can't grow on them.

In winter, snow blows to the leeward side of the dunes. Sand blows over the snow, forming ice cells which remain buried and frozen until summer, when they melt into ponds between the dunes. Some of the smaller ponds resemble quicksand. The Tri-Territory Loop road will lead you to the Killpecker Sand Dunes parking lot. Be careful where you drive off-road, because cars sometimes get stuck here.

You can see lots of wildlife in the Red Desert. Both Cedar Canyon and White Mountain have Indian petroglyphs which are easy to get to. In early summer you can see dozens of varieties of wildflowers.

Boar's Tusk, a desert landmark, is one of only two volcanic "necks" (cores) in this state. The other is Devils Tower, site of the movie, *Close Encounters of the Third Kind*. Lava from ancient volcanos is now mined as potash.

Sixty million years ago southwestern Wyoming was covered by a fresh-water lake now known as Lake Gosiute. Fossils abound here, in the desert and even next to the Interstate.

Even though it may seem to tourists that southwestern Wyoming has few attractions, people who live here say they could devote a lifetime to exploring the Red Desert, and still not tire of it. And it's just twenty-nine miles from the Killpecker Sand Dunes parking lot to Rock Springs.

ꜱ

*Answer: Butch Cassidy and his "Hole-in-the-Wall" Gang held up a Union Pacific train at Tipton. They got away with just $50.40 but did three thousand dollars damage to the railroad.

When they stopped to divide the proceeds, they discovered the three bags they had thought were filled with gold contained merely pennies. "They can't make us take that kind of money!" cried Harry Longabaugh, the Sundance Kid, and he poured the pennies down a prairie dog hole.

Indian petroglyphs in two locations in the Red Desert are easily accessible.

About the Close-Up
•• Don't tell Dick Randall the Red Desert is a wasteland. He knows the desert—from years of killing its animals, and from years of trying to save them.

Close-Up: DICK RANDALL
IF YOU WERE TO TELL DICK Randall the Red Desert has nothing to offer, he just might agree with you.

"People tell me this is a vast wasteland, and I say, 'You're right—and if you don't have money to get out of the state, I'll help you.'

"I like it the way it is. It's not desolate, it's wonderful. I get back to Washington D.C. pretty often, and occasionally New York, and I love to be a tourist there for about a week. And then I get crazy and have to get back to the hills."

Randall, a native Wyomingite, has herded sheep, cow-punched, run a cafe and service station, worked as diesel mechanic, led pack trips, made gas-powered fireplace logs, and ridden horseback over a ninety-mile area for a utility company sniffing for gas leaks.

Now he is an advocate for the Red Desert—and for its wildlife. But for ten years Randall made his living killing animals suspected of preying on livestock. He once shot forty-six coyotes in six hours, gunning them down from an airplane during a winter storm. In one month he killed two hundred thirty coyotes, a state record. In five months he killed seven hundred four. He worked for two federal agencies: Animal Damage Control and the U.S. Fish and Wildlife Service.

"At the time I thought I was doing the right thing, helping the agricultural industry," Randall said. Gradually his feelings changed. He said the cruelty of the methods he used troubled him: stuffing burning sagebrush in coyotes' dens to suffocate the pups; leaving bears and bobcats to linger for days in leg-hold traps; poisoning coyotes with a "sub-lethal" dose which took weeks to kill them.

Even more disturbing were the indiscriminate killings of animals and the resulting damage to the ecosystem. He shot seven black bears one month; only one had killed a lamb. He doesn't know how many animals he killed in all, because most of them he poisoned, and he didn't see them die.

In 1973—five years after his fourth on-the-job airplane crash—Randall quit predator control. He "jumped the fence," and for the next twelve years, was field representative for Defenders of Wildlife. Then he signed on as part-time consultant for the U.S. Humane Society and as volunteer for a half-dozen conservation groups.

His Rock Springs home is filled with awards. His work has been noted in the U.S. *Congressional Record*, and has been featured on national public television and in *U.S. News and World Report*.

Dick Randall knows the Red Desert—from years of killing its animals and from years of trying to save them.

Photography is Randall's first love—and photography is his most potent weapon in his campaign to stop the wide-scale animal killing which he now calls "futile." His picture of two bobcats caught in a trap was chosen for a U.S. Humane Society poster. His howling coyote became the national emblem for Defenders of Wildlife.

"Photography is what I like to do the most, but it seems my purpose in life over the last fourteen or fifteen years is to be a troublemaker," Randall said.

A graduate of the Arizona School of Photography, Randall documented his predator killings with his Hasselblad camera, and he now gives public showings of those photographs. Some federal agency spokespersons say those pictures don't reflect present-day policies; Randall disagrees.

"If I went out tomorrow and took pictures of animals in leg-hold traps, I'd have exactly the same photos I took twenty years ago.

"The cheapest way to kill massive amounts of wildlife is with poison," said Randall. "There's no such thing as selective poisoning. We kill hundreds and hundreds of bald eagles, golden eagles. Some poisons are targeted for canines, but then you're saying that all coyotes are guilty [of killing livestock]. They're not. Let's take out the guilty animals instead of making war on a whole species."

A photograph of one coyote Randall killed and dissected shows nineteen field mice inside the animal. "And I killed him with tax dollars for predator control. God, think of the good he was doing! At the same time I killed this coyote, the federal government was spending money for rodent control.

"Coyotes are wonderful rodent catchers. They're good grasshopper catchers. In 1967 we hurt the coyote population terribly, and when we killed off the coyotes, we completely changed the ecosystem. Now raccoons and red foxes have started moving in from Nebraska, and they are hell on water fowl."

In the past, Animal Damage Control didn't concern itself with the ecosystem, Randall said, but now public protest is bringing about change. "Taxpayers are seeing their millions and millions of dollars going to kill animals. The more people learn about it, the more responsible D.C. is going to have to become.

"We need to protect livestock instead of killing wildlife. We should have some handle on verified predation. What we need is a two- to three-year study by a third party. How many animals are lost to coyotes? Bears? Foxes?

"A good portion of the predation would never happen if you had a good sheepherder, but it's very difficult to hire a good sheepherder when the pay is only five hundred to six hundred dollars a month for a seven-day week. It's a tough job with no time off."

Randall herded sheep one summer in an area with a lot of coyotes. "I lost two or three sheep all summer out of a herd of twelve hundred. But I put a lot of time in, too.

"The desert lends itself to sheep use much more than cattle," Randall said, "but so many sheepmen today are turning to cattle. As soon as the cows are turned loose, they're heading for the nearest water hole and wallowing in the water. They're destroying the riparian habitat.

"I'm not an advocate of getting all the livestock off the public land, but I do think there ought to be more concern for the habitat. If you lose the habitat, you lose the wildlife. Our desert is so damn fragile. Wherever it's overgrazed, you cause a huge amount of erosion.

"There are some good ranchers out there—and some s.o.b.s who shouldn't be allowed livestock on public land," said Randall. "At Vermillion Creek on Pine Mountain a rancher comes in and blasts out the beaver dams. Then he switches from sheep to cows. Vermillion Creek used to have brook trout. Now it's become a gully because cows have denuded the creek.

"With the cows, they don't have anyone herding them. So the next thing, the rancher builds a fence. In the winter antelope gather in herds of eight hundred to a thousand. They migrate, depending on the weather and on their feed. Antelope don't do well with fences; they die of exhaustion trying to jump them. To kill off the antelope for the sake of somebody's cattle allotment? No! No! Not on public land.

"I think ranchers should be a bit responsible. There are some awfully bad problems with management, and politics enter in so much. Ranchers carry a lot of weight when it comes to not changing what they're doing.

"There's no panacea for predation, but there are some things that can help. Ranchers could use guard dogs. In pasture areas they could use electric fences. Some people are putting llamas out with their sheep. The llamas run coyotes off.

"In Canada, they're using aversives. Anything that dies in the winter, they'll bone it, grind it up, wrap it in a lamb pelt and inject it with lithium chloride. The coyote eats this, and it makes him deathly sick. He associates this with the lamb skin. They're having pretty good success with this, but aversives wouldn't work on open range. On open range you need good sheepherders.

"You're not going to wipe out the coyotes," said Randall. "They're so adaptable—and I respect them so much. If you were looking for a job that would last forever, predator control would be it. The futility of it all! I'd go out every year and do the same thing. Bang! Bang!"

Today Randall takes groups camping in the Red Desert. He shows them the wildlife, from wild horses to salamanders. He takes them to living sand dunes, aspen groves, and volcanic rock formations such as Honeycomb Buttes.

"There are minerals in there—layers and layers of minerals. If you get a rain there, oh! it's the most beautiful thing! It looks as if they've painted it.

"A lot of people think the desert is just a vast wasteland, there's nothing there. It's one of the few places left that there is something there—that's still like it was hundreds of years ago. It's such a beautiful place—and it has to be preserved."

৵

Chapter 11

Rock Springs

ROCK SPRINGS, Wyoming's fourth largest town
Population 19,050   *Elevation 6,271*
*Question: How did Butch Cassidy get his name?

Places to Visit

•• Chamber of Commerce and Information Center, 1897 Dewar Drive. Take Dewar Drive exit south. Center is on right side of street.

•• Western Wyoming College on College Drive. WWC has a natural history museum, art gallery, a giant pendulum, and dinosaur reproductions. An exact replica of an Easter Island statue stands on the back parking lot, acquired through the efforts of archaeologist-geologist Charlie Love. The main campus building, designed so faculty and students can get from classroom to classroom without going outside, won awards for its architecture. You can see 140 miles from the college grounds, including the Wind River Mountains to the north and the Uinta Mountains to the southwest.

•• Wild horse corrals behind Bureau of Land Management office off Highway 191 just north of town (take Elk Street exit). Ask for directions at BLM office on right side of highway.

•• Restored coal tipple at Reliance, northeast of town off Highway 191.

•• Rock Springs Historical Museum, Broadway at B Street.
•• Sweetwater Community Fine Arts Center, 400 C Street.

A Brief Background

Rock Springs has the most diverse population of any place between Los Angeles and Chicago. Descendants of at least fifty-seven nations live here. International Night, held each June, celebrates the community's global heritage.

The town began in the 1860s as a stage stop on the Overland Trail. Travelers passing through town carved their names on rocks, which now stand behind private homes.

The white streaks in the rocks surrounding the city are oil shale. Wyoming has enough oil deposits to supply the United States for three hundred years, but currently, extracting it would be too expensive to be feasible.

Coal was Rock Springs's main resource. The city is built over coal mine shafts, and this sometimes causes problems for property owners. Residents tell of buildings sinking five or six feet, of pets being rescued from mine shafts, and of house basements flooding because abandoned mine shafts have filled with water. The umbrella term for these problems is subsidence (sub-sye-dence), a form of the word subside, meaning to settle.

Coal mines displaced the springs Rock Springs was named for. The water which filled the mines was pumped into Bitter Creek, and the springs went dry. Now that the Rock Springs mines are abandoned, some springs are beginning to come back.

The Wyoming Coal and Mining Company opened mines at Rock Springs in 1868 to provide coal for the Union Pacific Railroad. Most of the earliest miners here came from the British Isles and eastern United States. They lived in dugouts carved into the banks of Bitter Creek or in railroad box cars. Later Union Pacific provided company housing.

Union Pacific took over the mines in 1874, and under Jay Gould's leadership, reduced the miners' pay. When workers protested, Gould replaced them with Chinese miners willing to work for less. By 1880, 497 of Rock Springs's 763 residents were Chinese. They declined to join the newly formed Knights of Labor, viewing this as an exclusive white men's club. Besides, most of them hoped to return to China as soon as they could afford to, so going on strike for better long-term conditions was contrary to their needs.

Other miners perceived the Chinese as gaining the best housing and the best working conditions from Union Pacific. Resentments festered.

On September 2, 1885, white miners burned the Chinese section of town, killing twenty-eight Chinese residents and wounding fifteen. The survivors fled to Evanston, then returned to Rock Springs under the protection of federal troops, who occupied Rock Springs at the hastily constructed Camp Pilot Butte, adjacent to Chinatown, until the Spanish-American War.

The Chinese massacre drew national attention. President Grover Cleveland issued a statement decrying it. As a result, Union Pacific altered its practices in two ways:

• It brought in equipment that required fewer workers.

• It recruited miners from many nations and housed them side by side, assuming that if they didn't speak the same language they couldn't unionize.

That plan didn't work; shared conditions brought the miners together. They lived in crude company houses and shopped in the company store with scrip they received as pay. Once electricity became available, houses had one light bulb each, and company officials checked to see that miners didn't turn it on during the day. Lawns and trees were forbidden because of the water shortage. Union Pacific hauled water from Green River to use in the mines.

If you drive around old Rock Springs, on the north side of the tracks, you will see some of the old Union Pacific two-room houses. The long, narrow ones were called "shotgun" houses—if you were to fire a charge through the front door, it would go straight through the house and out the back.

The north side of town also has social halls where immigrants met with others from their native lands. The Finns were the most radical in their politics, and for years Wyoming law forbade marriage between Finns and other Wyomingites.

In 1907, three hundred Japanese miners joined their Caucasian co-workers in a strike against Union Pacific. The Rock Springs miners were the first to invite Asians to join United Mine Workers of America. Striking workers closed down all the Rock Springs mines so that Union Pacific was forced to negotiate, and southern Wyoming mines became unionized.

Union Pacific closed the last of its Rock Springs mines in the mid-fifties, after converting its railroad engines to diesel power. They offered company houses for sale for one hundred dollars, but they removed all necessary services, such as electricity and water. Even the post office had been run from the company store. The town survived partly because trona mines west of Green River had opened by then.

During the energy boom of the 1970s, Rock Springs gained notoriety when CBS dubbed it "Sin City" during two *60 Minutes* exposés. Residents admit that the population explosion brought housing crises, impacted classrooms, and a rise in crime, but say that most of the crime was confined to downtown K Street and that their home neighborhoods remained safe. They point out, too, that many of those who moved to Rock Springs during the boom years became an asset to the community, and that without these progressive newcomers, Rock Springs might never have passed bonds to build their community college and recreation centers.

The early seventies were frantic times. Police dispatch calls for Rock Springs increased from nine thousand in 1970 to one hundred thousand in 1974. School enrollment more than doubled. One woman reported that when she registered her son for first grade in 1973, during the middle of the school year, he was one of eight new children enrolling in his class that day.

Rock Springs survived the boom and the bust which followed. Mining is still Rock Springs's chief source of employment: trona mining west of Green River and coal mining east of Rock Springs. Townspeople take pride in their sense of community, their excellent schools and recreation facilities, their nearness to wide open spaces, and their ability to survive booms and busts.

⌐

*Butch Cassidy, born Robert Leroy Parker, took on the name of an old southern Utah outlaw named Mike Cassidy when he was a teenager. He became "Butch" Cassidy when he went to work for a butcher shop on North Front Street in Rock Springs.

About The Close-Ups

•• Miners are every bit as interesting as ranchers and cowboys, says Dudley Gardner. And they have contributed more to Wyoming's economy than any other group.

••How can people protect wild horses without losing them, and other wildlife, because of overpopulation? There is no perfect answer, says Don Schramm, assistant manager of the Bureau of Land Management office north of Rock Springs.

Close-Up: A. DUDLEY GARDNER

DUDLEY GARDNER IS A HISTORIAN, archaeologist, and instructor at Western Wyoming College. He led the campaign to restore

Historian Dudley Gardner says miners are every bit as interesting as ranchers and cowboys.

the tipple at the abandoned coal mine at Reliance, helped restore Rock Springs City Hall, and is in charge of archaeological digs at Fort Bridger. He and his wife, Jodi, have restored an abandoned house in their back yard which was once owned by the Union Pacific Railroad and rented to miners.

Gardner is author, with Verla Flores, of *Forgotten Frontier: A History of Wyoming Coal Mining,* and co-authored, with Val Brinkerhoff, *An American Place: A Centennial Portrait of Rock Springs, Wyoming.* He is currently working on a history of Asians in Wyoming.

Gardner has conducted hundreds of oral interviews during the eleven years he has lived in Rock Springs, and many of these are quoted in part in *Forgotten Frontier.* The book stirred controversy in *New Republic* magazine because of Gardner's "radical" approach to history.

"If it is radical, it was that we focused on the common people," Gardner said. "The common people speak through oral history.

"Coal mining gives a richness and a depth to our history that few understand," said Gardner. "Miners contributed more than any other single group to Wyoming's economy. I think they really have been overlooked. Twenty-five per cent of our state's economy depends on mining and only two per cent on farming and ranching. Some guy said that you either grow it or you dig it out of the ground, and in this place you don't grow it."

Of the more than one hundred silent movies made in Wyoming, none was about miners, Gardner noted. "Coal mining seems mundane and commonplace. But on wagon trains the routine was boring too. If you can make someone riding on a horse, eaten by mosquitoes, and pestered by flies glamorous, you can make coal miners glamorous." Coal miners were independent people with rich personalties, Gardner said. "Inside their room [in the mine] they were their own boss."

One reason for the dearth of information about Wyoming coal miners is that few left journals. Another is that "coal mining is seen as disruptive and extractive," Gardner said. "Gold is romantic—coal is not. But to smelt gold you needed coal."

A drawback Gardner sees to mining as a career is its boom-bust character. He says mining companies don't always make that pattern clear to people when they recruit. "They'll move people out here and tell them, 'You've got 30 years' work. That's how long the mine's going to last.' It gives people false hope. Mines open—mines close. It's a Western pattern. That's a fact of life.

"You invest money in a house, live in the house for two years, the mine goes belly-up. The big corporation can take these losses as a tax deduction, but you can't.

"Government subsidies aren't the answer. There'll always be corporate managers who don't plan ahead. They'd better not promise people anything they can't deliver.

"I think the common person has always been taken advantage of, and the only option he has when the mines close is to move. The old-timers always look to see how long you're going to last. Can you last out the next bust? That's the real test."

Close-Up: ROCK SPRINGS HORSE CORRALS

WHAT CAN BE A MORE BEAUTIFUL sight than herds of horses running free? One would think that wild horses must be one of Wyoming's most treasured resources, for their power and grace alone.

But the horses pose a problem to this fragile desert environment. They have adapted so well, their numbers are increasing by about twenty per cent per year. Too many horses mean not enough vegetation will remain for all the wildlife and livestock in the desert—not even for the horses themselves.

In this land of few fences, horses range freely on privately owned ranches and on government grazing land leased by ranchers for their cattle and sheep. Unlike antelope, elk and deer, horses don't migrate from season to season.

"Horses eat out areas," said Don Schramm, assistant manager of the Bureau of Land Management office north of Rock Springs. "We make ranchers rotate their livestock. But with wild horses, we're allowing year-round grazing.

"We're finding out these horses do what they want. They don't migrate, they don't distribute. They bunch up—they'll stay in an area where they've got water. They're destroying the range in one area. We need to do something—get them rotated."

The BLM rounds up six hundred to a thousand horses a year—around Rock Springs, Rawlins, and Worland—transports them to corrals just north of Rock Springs and offers

Wild horses and the BLM roundups are an emotional issue. These horses are in corral behind Bureau of Land Management office.

them for adoption. The agency has kept the size of the herd stable in that way. Wyoming has about three thousand wild horses, Schramm said. Nevada, in contrast, has thirty-five thousand.

BLM workers capture horses year-round except during the coldest winter months and during foaling season, April through June. The summer months from July on are a good time to visit the corral. Be forewarned, though. These horses are wild and scared, and they will bite and kick if given a chance.

The BLM rounds up the horses by helicopter, herding them a maximum of seven or eight miles into enclosures constructed of jute matting strung on six-foot poles. Wranglers then run the horses into portable corrals. They limit their catch to one truckload—about forty horses—per day.

Herding wild horses isn't like herding cattle. It's dangerous work; wranglers may get kicked, bitten, and run over. "Everybody feels like they're qualified to be a horse wrangler," Schramm said. "But it's not like rodeoing, not like being a cowhand." Wild horse wranglers need exceptional riding, roping, and horse-handling skills.

After they have been transferred to the Rock Springs corrals, the horses are identified by age, sex, height and weight, color, markings, and where and when they were captured. A veterinarian examines and vaccinates them before they are registered for adoption. A few select horses are returned to the range to improve the herd.

Hardly any of the horses are adopted by Rock Springs residents. The majority go to homes east of the Mississippi, Schramm said. "We catch them, work them, identify them, and send them to other BLM facilities in the East." The BLM also holds weekend horse shows in nearby states, trucking some fifty horses at a time to a sale barn or rodeo arena where the public can select them.

The BLM retains ownership of the horses for a year after they are adopted, to prevent new owners from selling them or using them in an inhumane way. "We try to get them interested in the horses' needs as well as theirs," one staff member said. "You don't go out and buy a lion just because you think it's cute. I feel the same about horses."

The 125 dollar adoption fee covers about one-fourth of the BLM's cost, Schramm said. "We're talking about a fifty-dollar bill to catch a horse. It's after we get them into the corral that it gets expensive."

Until recently, horses not chosen for adoption—usually studs nine years or older—were shipped to a sanctuary in South Dakota. The BLM paid a dollar and twenty-five cents per horse per day, with the understanding that after three years the sanctuary would draw enough private donations to become self-supporting. That didn't happen, Schramm said, and the sanctuary cannot continue operating. This means that unadopted horses will either be returned to the range or be offered for sale for slaughter and other commercial uses.

Schramm believes that returning older horses to the range wouldn't be feasible because of their numbers and the way they would skew the composition of the herd.

"[People] harvest deer and they harvest antelope," Schramm said. "To me it's unrealistic to say that the BLM is going to remove all cattle from the range and have only horses. We're in the livestock business, we're not running a zoo. And even zoos don't keep more than two elephants.

"It's an emotional issue."

⌁

Chapter 12

Green River

GREEN RIVER, Wyoming's seventh largest town
Population 12,711   *Elevation 6,100*
*Question: What does Seedskadee mean?

Places to Visit

•• Expedition Island, launching site for John Wesley Powell's tour down the Green, Grand, and Colorado rivers—and a good place to picnic. Take I-80 Business Route and follow the signs.

•• Seedskadee National Wildlife Refuge, nine miles west on I-80, then twenty-eight miles north on Highway 372. The refuge has more than two hundred species of birds, including all those native to Wyoming.

•• Flaming Gorge National Recreation Area, about seventy miles south of Green River. Stop at visitors' center on Highway 530 south of town.

A Brief Background

Those rocks which line the Interstate near the Green River exits are the Palisades. You may have seen them in paintings by Thomas Moran. Castle Rock is the one most often pictured.

Green River is county seat of Sweetwater County, gateway to Flaming Gorge National Recreation Area, and the closest

181

community to five trona mines. Some trona miners live in company housing here and ride company buses to work.

Green River also has a thirty-track railroad yard and three hundred railroad employees. The town's first settlers arrived a few months before the railroad did, in 1868. They claimed to have a land grant from Congress, but railroad officials declared the settlers were on Union Pacific property and demanded they pay for their lots.

The settlers said they would pay only if Union Pacific promised to make Green River its stopping place for the winter. The railroad's response was to found a new town, Bryan, twelve miles west. Nearly everyone in Green River moved to Bryan then, to work on the railroad. But Bryan ran short of water, so Union Pacific returned to Green River in 1872. The railroad used its roundhouse here until after World War II.

The Green River Ordinance, regulating door-to-door salesmen, began here in 1931 so night shift railroad employees wouldn't have their sleep disturbed.

In 1957 the Bureau of Reclamation started construction on the Flaming Gorge Dam on the Green River, thirty-two miles downstream from the Wyoming-Utah border. The dam was completed in 1963. First Lady Ladybird Johnson came to Green River in 1964 and made the Flaming Gorge Dam dedication speech in front of the Sweetwater County Courthouse.

The dam, 530 feet high, provides hydroelectric power for Wyoming, Utah, Colorado, and New Mexico.

Flaming Gorge Reservoir covered up the town of Linwood, Wyoming. The reservoir is ninety-one miles long, and the national area surrounding it encompasses part of Wyoming and Utah.

Highway 530 south is the most popular route to Flaming Gorge. The lake is famous for trout, kokanee, and bass fishing. Diving is popular, and wet suits are recommended, since

Flaming Gorge Reservoir, which is a good camping and fishing area, covered up the town of Linwood, Wyoming.

the surface water rarely gets above sixty-eight degrees Fahrenheit. Deeper water temperatures are colder.

Some people come to the gorge to sight-see and tour the dam. Some take raft trips down the Green River. The recreation area has hiking and bike trails, picnic areas, campgrounds, and a lookout tower open to the public. If you come camping with a group, you will need a reservation. Individual campsites sometimes fill in the summer, but usually people can camp in overflow areas.

Fishing at Flaming Gorge is open year-round (ice fishing in winter). The recreation area also has cross-country ski and snowmobile trails.

From Flaming Gorge you can take Highway 43 out of Manila, Utah, west, then north forty miles into Mountain View, then go six miles north through Bridger Valley to rejoin the Interstate.

Some tourists take a scenic loop: south on Highway 191 out of Rock Springs, west on Highway 44, and then north on Highway 530 to Green River. Some turn off Highway 191 near the Wyoming-Utah border and drive twenty-two miles east to Brown's Park, where Old West outlaws used to hang out.

If you stay on Interstate 80 from Green River to Bridger Valley, you will come to Holding's Little America: a place to stop for the night, get bargain ice cream cones, buy gasoline, and more. The founder was marooned here during a blizzard and vowed if he survived, he would build a center for travelers at this spot. Some employees say that contrary to popular belief, Holding wasn't the founder: that Holding took over after the founder went bankrupt.

Near Little America, roads lead north to five plants where more than three thousand employees mine and process trona. Trona is soda ash, used mainly for glass, detergents, paper, aluminum, and agricultural products. It is less porous and less flammable than coal, but the processes used in mining trona are similar to those of coal mining.

The five Wyoming mines produce twenty-five per cent of the world's soda ash. An estimated two hundred billion tons of trona has yet to be mined here—enough to supply the United States for three thousand years. Compared to trona reserves elsewhere, these are relatively easy to mine, and this makes the price competitive on the world market.

Largest of the five plants is FMC Corporation, which has more than twenty-five hundred miles of streets in its underground mines—more streets than the entire City of San Francisco has.

Trona mines provide employment not only to Green River and Rock Springs residents, but also to those in Bridger Valley, our next stopping point.

ᘔ

*Answer: Seedskadee is the Shoshone name for the Green River. It means "River of the Sage Chicken."

About the Close-Ups

•• One of the most celebrated journeys in Western history is Major John Wesley Powell's excursion down the Green, Grand, and Colorado rivers. It started from Expedition Island in Green River.

•• Herb Price, mining superintendent at Texas-Gulf Trona, believes corporations need to make the welfare of their employees and consumers top priority—not dollars. Read what else he believes.

•• Stan Owens comes from a family of miners and railroad workers. Owens shows us that trona mines can be a good place to work.

•• It took courage for women to work underground, after centuries of superstition that women brought bad luck. It took courage to stay—as Barbara Miller has—for more than fifteen years. Now she enjoys her job, despite its drawbacks.

Close-Up: JOHN WESLEY POWELL

ON MAY 24, 1864, TEN MEN embarked from Expedition Island on a ninety-nine day journey down the Green, Grand, and Colorado rivers. They left in three twenty-one-foot oaken boats plus a sixteen-foot pilot boat of pine, christened *Emma Dean* in honor of John Wesley Powell's wife.

Major Powell, a thirty-five-year-old Methodist minister's son who had lost his right arm in the Civil War, was a former country school teacher and principal and self-taught naturalist.

He had never completed college, but had nevertheless become Professor of Geology at two Illinois universities and Curator of the Illinois Natural History Society.

Powell's party consisted of four trappers, a former printer, Powell's brother, who was still recovering from the Civil War, an eighteen-year-old vagabond, an Englishman in search of adventure, and an army sergeant willing to do nearly anything to get out of the military. Only the Powell brothers and the sergeant had passed their thirtieth birthdays.

The expedition was financed by a meager Congressional appropriation of goods and services plus eleven hundred dollars from the Illinois universities where Powell had taught. None of the crew was paid except for the trappers.

For the first thirty days no one heard from the explorers, and rumors circulated that the ten men had drowned in the Green River rapids. Actually, the only casualties by then were one of the boats and its contents—and the morale of the men.

Powell's caution and his meticulousness in making and recording observations irritated his crew. The expedition was so poorly funded, sometimes the men didn't have enough food. Danger lay around every bend: each set of rapids seemed more treacherous than the one before. The Englishman left the expedition after a month, walking thirty miles from the mouth of the Uinta River to civilization.

By August 28 the party had made its way into the Grand Canyon. There the printer and two of the trappers decided they could no longer face the river's perils, so they climbed out of the canyon, after wishing the other men well. The three were almost immediately killed by Shivwit Indians. Two days later, the six remaining crew members completed their river journey near what is now Lake Mead.

Powell returned to Illinois, then boarded the train for Washington D.C. where he received a hero's welcome. He led some additional expeditions and in 1870 was appointed Director of the U.S. Geographical and Geological Survey of the Rocky Mountain Region. Later he became director of both the U.S. Geological Survey and of the Bureau of Ethnology, a branch of the Smithsonian Institution.

Powell bucked popular opinion by declaring that western lands lacked water, and that only twenty per cent of the lands west of the one hundredth meridian could be reclaimed through irrigation. (The one hundredth meridian passes through North Dakota, South Dakota, Nebraska, Kansas, Oklahoma, and Texas.)

He promoted reform of homestead acts whereby irrigable land grants would be limited to eighty acres instead of the usual one hundred sixty, and dry pasture homesteads would be increased to 2,560 acres. He also advocated the federal government's specifying where pioneers would be allowed to homestead and controlling the water available to them, to avoid their settling upstream and diverting the water before it could benefit the most people.

Congress appropriated funds in 1888 for Powell to conduct an irrigation survey, and it repealed existing land laws west of the one hundredth meridian until the survey could be completed. But in 1890, impatient with the time the survey required, Congress reversed itself and rejected Powell's recommendations—recommendations which today's Western water specialists say made good sense.

Close-Up: HERB PRICE

HERB PRICE APPEARS EQUALLY comfortable explaining the mechanics of short-wall mining fourteen hundred feet underground, and leading a classroom discussion on Maslov's hierarchy of needs. As mine superintendent at Texas-Gulf Trona, he concerns himself with all aspects of mining, including the

Mining superintendent Herb Price believes the welfare of employees and consumers needs to be a top priority.

welfare of his work force. He teaches a class on supervision at Western Wyoming College's Green River campus.

Price believes that how people get along on the job depends largely on management's priorities. "The biggest problem with management in this country today is not having and expressing the proper values. If our Number One priority is dollars, this is going to have a very negative effect on employee safety.

"We have to talk about our values, to be very clear in our own minds about what is important. Otherwise, we're sort of lost."

Price admits that dollars are important. "If you don't make a profit, you don't stay in business." But he believes businesses are better off in the long-run if they put the well-being of their employees and customers first—and if they do this in a non-authoritarian way.

"Authoritarianism is a kind of disease, in that we get trapped in it. People get frozen into not being able to do anything that the organization doesn't direct to get done. They won't do anything innovative without the blessing of someone above them. If you try to move them out of that with authority, you continue the same problem. It's a Catch-22—like saying, 'We're going to have an enlightened management here, and anyone that doesn't get on the bandwagon is out!'

"People don't want to do something because the manager says so, to satisfy someone's ego, but they will work for the betterment of the organization. Most of the people who work here are very cooperative."

Price has been at the Green River site since 1970, when the company began its test mining there. Construction of the mine and refining plants began in 1973.

"You can't run a mine without having some rigidity—we have to have some common procedures. But we try to let crews have as much freedom as they can. If you have too many rules, it causes people to want to defy those rules in ways that they get into trouble. I believe the higher the level of authoritarianism, the more disorder you have."

The founders of Texas-Gulf took a "paternalistic" attitude toward its employees, Price said, and tried to protect them "from womb to tomb."

"They thought that very high benefits would keep people happy, and they wouldn't feel the need to move on. You don't want your work force worrying about losing their income, but I don't see that as a replacement for meeting people's aspirations.

"Most people go to work in a job like this to put bread on the table. We talk about menial work as being boring-type work. A lot of our work is repetitive. If that's all there is, if it's only come, do as you're told, go home every day—that's negative; it's boring; it will come to show on people.

"The internal drive comes from being allowed to make one's own decisions and to be creative—finding new and better ways to do things to make the job easier, safer, or to bring about cost savings. How well do we do in that area? Fair, at best.

"Our tolerance for non-conformity in this country is not very high. I'd like to have the highest level of decision-making, the highest level of creativity, of autonomy. But when you're working with a crew of people, where safety is a concern, you have to conform a certain amount."

Texas-Gulf Trona is a non-union mine. "Almost everybody here has worked under a union at one time, but we've never had a union election. Our pay is as good as anybody else's and our benefits are as good or better. There's a bitterness that so often goes on in labor relations. It's better when people try to get along, rather than fighting over every little thing."

Poor management brings on the need for unions, Price said. "We've had a few things here that people have gotten riled up about. A couple of years ago we had a reduction in force, probably at one of the worst times it could have been done. When people see management do things that seem nonsensical, they feel powerless. At least, with a union you get some power."

Texas-Gulf Trona has 133 underground mine employees, and a total of 320 working in the mine, in administration, and in the refining plant. Turnover at the mine averages two or three employees a year.

As for safety: the average incidence rate for mines nationwide—those on-the-job injuries which require medical attention—is eight per two hundred thousand work-hours. "Our incidence rate right now is a little over four, which is high. We'd like to have it zero."

"Mining is kind of fun," said Price. "You're in a rock that probably no one else has ever seen, that's fifty million years old; there's an element of discovery.

"You do see something change and move, and it's fun to run heavy equipment. And I suspect people really enjoy doing things that are of benefit to society."

Some people criticize all mining as being "extractive," and thus harmful to the environment. "People who do not see the human values involved in using the earth's minerals— they're neurotic," Price said. "It's a fanaticism that isn't beneficial to society or themselves."

Close-Up: STAN OWENS

STAN OWENS HAS BEEN MINING ever since he graduated from high school in 1974. He works the maintenance shift at Texas-Gulf Trona.

"I'm a jack-of-all-trades, really. I go in with the mechanics, and I set up for the production people coming in on the next shift. I go in and I take the rail down, pull back the cables, and if the roof gets bad I bolt it up.

"I usually work by myself, but there's other people around me. There's somebody in the general vicinity, just in case somebody gets hurt. I go in and do what needs to be done."

The first few years Owens worked at Stauffer Chemical Company (now Rhone-Poulenc.) He had uncles working there who helped him get a job. "I was a grievance man at Stauffer. When we had lay-offs, I had to go down and inform people. It was hard."

One of his brothers still works at Rhone-Poulenc. Another brother is a miner at FMC, and his sister works at Texas-Gulf, in trafficking.

Owens was born and raised in Green River. His dad was a foreman on the Union Pacific Railroad for fifty-five years,

Trona miner Stan Owens comes from a family of miners and railroad workers.

and one of his brothers is a railroad engineer. While Owens was growing up, his uncle was chief of police in Green River.

He started college in Nebraska, but he stayed there only a week. He came back to Green River and married a hometown girl. They have six children.

"It's been a good life. I really like mining. Wages are good—but the cost of living is high, too." He hasn't ever considered doing another kind of work, he said. "It's all I know.

"I'd like to learn something else, in case they ever had a lay-off. The company will pay for our schooling as long as it's work-related. The opportunity's there, if I'd just do it."

He said the mine superintendent told him that Texas-Gulf's trona reserves should keep miners employed from fifty to ninety years. "So some of us will have a good chance to retire here."

"I've been a downshift maintenance person since I was hired on," Owens said. "For a year I went over and ran a miner while we cut out a section. I'd rather be downshifting." Running a miner is noisy. He wore ear plugs all the time.

Texas-Gulf is the only one of the Green River trona mines that shuts down on weekends, although the processing plant runs seven days a week. "That makes it real nice," Owens said.

He changes shifts each week. "That has its benefits. Days are fine because you see the kids after school. Swings are good—I get some stuff done at the house. Graveyards—you're numb all the time."

None of his children has visited the mine. His wife went down into Stauffer Chemical years ago and doesn't want to go into a mine again. She worries that Owens will get hurt.

"Nobody wants to get hurt. You try to be careful. If you hear a loud bang, you know you should walk away real fast."

The company provides respirators and requires workers to wear them when they are dry roof bolting or driving the miner. "A lot of people say they go overboard on safety here, but it's for your own protection. Trona is water-soluble, but when you're roof bolting you hit oil shale, and that can damage your lungs. You should wear your respirator on the cars, too. You're a dummy if you don't."

Owens wears a respirator when he is around the diesel cars and wherever it is dusty. "If you breathe a lot of trona, you nose will start bleeding."

Owens is a member of one of the company's two rescue teams. "If there's ever a mine disaster, we're trained to go down and get the people out. We wear self-contained breathing apparatus."

He applied to be on the team, and then other members voted him in. "They do it that way because they figure you've got to put your life on the line with that person." The team will respond to a disaster, such as a methane explosion, in any neighboring mine, too.

"Methane explosions are not common in trona mines. Our equipment has a methane detector on it, and if it detects methane, it shuts off.

"They say that trona mines are really somewhat fireproof. Coal burns, but trona doesn't. And our equipment has fire retardant on it." Nationwide, more fatalities have occurred in the trona processing plants than in the mines, Owens said—people getting hurt on conveyor belts or running trucks over cliffs. Down below, people are safety-conscious.

"I brought a couple of guys down on a tour. One of them heard a ping on the short wall and wanted to leave real fast.

"Some people have a hard time handling the cage ride going down: that sudden looking over, seeing through the grating. There are so many checks, everything has to be going right for the cage [elevator] to run. They were having trouble with it for awhile, where it would stop part way down. If anything's not quite right, they put it in low, run it at half-speed, so it takes four minutes to go down instead of two.

"Being a trona miner is a lot nicer than being a coal miner, from what I understand. We're clean. It's just like working in a warehouse. An office building has littler hallways than where I am in the mine, and I have more working space than they do in those little desk cubicles in the office.

"The work I'm doing now I really enjoy. It's different and challenging. I like coming out and working, seeing how much I can get done. I like the accomplishment of coming out and doing something—just having a job. Especially in these times."

Close-Up: **BARBARA MILLER**

UNTIL THE LAST FEW DECADES, women underground were thought to bring bad luck. But during the 1970s some Wyoming women joined the mining work force, and a few of the hardier ones stayed. Barbara Miller has worked as electrician at Texas-Gulf Trona since 1976 and is the only woman currently working underground there.

"The first day I came here I didn't know anybody, and I was scared. I set my lunch bucket down on the table, and this guy takes it and throws it across the room. He says, 'This is where I sit.'

"The next day there's tampons hanging all over the place, spray-painted red. Guys are lining up in front of me to take a leak in the rib [wall]. 'Welcome to T-G, Barbara.'

"The idea was to get rid of me. I got told real often I had no business here. This was a place for a man, and I was taking a man's job away from him. I told them if the man I'd married had been a man, I wouldn't have to be here.

"I was divorced and raising two kids. You can't do that on women's wages. Where I went to high school, in Riverton, girls took secretarial courses. We weren't allowed to take shop. They told us we'd all get married and stay home and raise our families. Why did they lie to us?

"Before I came to work here I took classes in underground mining at Western Wyoming College. My mechanics teacher told me about the job at Texas-Gulf.

"He was so nasty to me in class—he sent me home bawling so many times! At the end of the year he told me, 'You say you want to work in a mine. What I wanted to teach you was how to take whatever they give you.' He also made me promise that if I took the job, I'd stay at least a year.

"That mechanics teacher of mine—he turned out to be the best thing that ever happened to me. You just learn not to

Barbara Miller had the courage to work underground even though the superstition was that women brought bad luck.

be so sensitive—and you'd better really want a job.

"One of the reasons I had so many problems here is they'd had other women working here they didn't like. They had another woman in my crew before I came. One night, when they were all working overtime, she climbed up on the table and told the guys she could take them all on. She was a hard act to follow.

"I started out at nine dollars an hour, twice as much as I'd been making at the telephone company. I thought I was in hog heaven. My job was to take care of the phones and pages underground. I got bored with that, so I started asking other electricians if I could follow them around and learn what they did.

"For some of the guys, it took a few weeks for them to accept me. For some it took a couple of years. It just depends on how you handle things. If you're going to go down there and act like a girl—that's what the guys call it—and get shocked at the language and shocked at who they are…. This is not my world, it's their world. You just learn not to be so sensitive.

"You make friends with the guys on your crew. The guy that I work with underground, he's probably my best friend. It's hard for a lot of people to understand that you can have a male friend. It's a case of proximity and getting to know someone. If you're a likable person, they're going to like you.

"Most women don't stay very long at the mines. It's dirty, it's hard work, it's heavy work. It's not like working in the office, where I could make friends I could see outside of work. I can't just take off and go to lunch with the girls.

"I have men that I talk to every day, that I have long discussions with, that don't say 'Good day' to me in the grocery store if they're with their wives. There are wives who treat me like some kind of leper. It can get real lonely.

"I left underground for awhile because a guy wouldn't keep his hands off me. We got called in to work one night and it got really bad. I had to take a two-grade cut to go on the surface. I worked in the mill for five years, doing electrical. I liked that a lot. I liked the fresh air on the surface, but I didn't like the cold.

"It's two different worlds. The guys that work in the mill think the guys underground are Neanderthal. The guys underground think the guys in the mill are pansy types. They're all just guys.

"I asked to go back underground because the foreman I had on the surface wouldn't leave me alone. T-G wasn't going to do anything to him unless I filed sexual harassment charges. I had to work here; I had two kids to raise. For me to bring charges would be out of the question. You can either want a job or not want a job—either play their game or not play their game.

"It's a lot more dangerous underground than on the surface. It's eighty per cent more dangerous. We had more accidents in the mill, but they were minor, like falling off a ladder and spraining an ankle, or breaking a leg. Underground the accidents are more serious.

"We have a guy who's been in the hospital for four years. He knows where he is, but he has no motor skills. A slab from the rib fell on him. You always worry about rib and roof control.

"You think about safety all the time, especially in my job. You're not working with one hundred ten, you're working with a thousand volts. Everybody looks out for everybody else. And it's an everyday, all-around-the-clock thing.

"We're a continuous miner mine, so we don't have to go in and blast. Our mine's a lot better than most mines. It's the second-best for safety. Rhone-Poulenc isn't nearly as deep as our mine, so their roof and rib control is easier.

"I have a bad back from working here. I'm a small person, and the belt we have to wear, with the self-rescuer, the lamp battery, it's heavy. It's hard on my back. Then there's the tools....

"I was off work three months because of my back. The doctor didn't want me to go back. I never missed anything as much as I missed this job!

"I want to do at least twenty years here. The doctor told me I'd never make it another five years—but I will. Then I want to go back to school. I bought some property near Medford, Oregon, and there's a good university near there. I want to study to be a counselor because I thinks kids really need help.

"Right now I've pretty much got it made. I'm as high a grade as I can go; my base salary is thirty-five hundred dollars a month. Those guys that harassed me are gone—but I'm still here.

"I have a good rapport with the guys underground. I don't think there's anybody underground that I can't work with or who doesn't say 'Good morning' to me. Now they tend to watch their language and they treat me pretty good.

"There are guys who are very protective of me. If somebody starts spreading stories about me most guys now say, 'Don't talk about her that way; she's not that way; we don't want to hear it.' And if I change my hair style, I hear about it from 150 men."

In September, 1991, Miller married a miner she had worked with for several years. "There are rules you go by: you don't date guys at your mine, you don't date guys in your crew. I broke the rules this time. I guess it's good that I did."

ॐ

Chapter 13
Bridger Valley

LYMAN	*Population 1,896*	*Elevation: 6,800 feet*
MOUNTAIN VIEW	*Population 1,189*	
FORT BRIDGER	*Population 100*	

*Question: Who was Thornburgh?

Places to Visit

•• Fort Bridger, the most visited state-owned historic site in Wyoming. In summer it features living history and moonlight tours. It is a good place to picnic, and admission is free. The fort is also known for its mountain man rendezvous held Labor Day weekend.

•• Wasatch National Forest in the Uinta Mountains, about 25 miles south of Mountain View, for uncrowded fishing, hiking, and camping in a scenic area. Camping rates range from no fee to five dollars per night.

•• Charcoal kilns at ghost town of Piedmont, built in 1868 to provide charcoal for the iron industry in Utah. The kilns, made of stone, are thirty feet high and thirty feet in diameter, and are listed in the National Register of Historic Places. Take Leroy exit off I-80 twelve miles west of Fort Bridger. Travel west to crossroads, then go south about 5 miles. A half-mile farther are remains of the town.

•• Trona museum at Lyman civic center.

A Brief Background

Bridger Valley is in Uinta County, named for the Uintah Indians. Some say Uintah means "healing waters," others say it means "land of the pines."

Shoshone Indians used to camp here. Their longtime leader Chief Washakie (1798-1900) is revered by both Indians and Euro-Americans. He believed in negotiating with settlers rather than attacking them, but he was sometimes disappointed in whites' failure to keep their word.

Jim Bridger (1804-1881), known as "Old Gabe" by Euro-Americans and as "Blanket Chief" by Crow Indians, came west from Missouri in 1822 with William Ashley's fur-trading expedition. Bridger trapped beaver, explored the West, and helped found the Rocky Mountain Fur Company. He discovered the Great Salt Lake when he was 20 and South Pass when he was 23.

He visited Yellowstone Lake and the geysers in 1830, but nobody believed his descriptions of them. Some think this is why Bridger became a notorious storyteller: since people didn't believe the truth, he might as well make up some tall tales. One of his most famous is about the petrified trees at Yellowstone, which Bridger said were filled with petrified birds singing petrified songs.

Bridger married a woman from the Flathead tribe and they had several children. After his first wife died in childbirth, Bridger married a Shoshone woman and fathered several more children.

When the beaver supply diminished and fashion turned to silk hats, Bridger set up a ferry to take emigrants on the Oregon Trail across the Green River and opened his trading post in 1842, with partner Luis Vasquez.

Mormon leader Brigham Young stopped by. He and Bridger clashed, and in 1853, after Young became Governor of the Territory and acting Indian agent, Young ordered his sheriff to seize Bridger's goods, arrest him, and bring him to Utah to stand trial for trading ammunition to the Shoshones so they could kill Mormons.

Bridger fled to Fort Laramie. The posse killed the Green River ferrymen, confiscated Bridger's livestock and merchandise, and set fire to the trading post. Some people say Bridger sold the trading post to Brigham Young, although Bridger denied this. Others say Bridger married a Mormon woman, who found him impossible to live with and soon left him. This seems unlikely.

Mormons operated the Fort Bridger trading post until 1857, when President Buchanan ordered federal troops to Utah to quell a rumored rebellion and to install a non-Mormon governor. Bridger hired on then as guide for the army. The army invasion ended peacefully, with President Buchanan sending Brigham Young a pardon and Young professing he didn't know what the pardon was for.

Both Fort Supply, a Mormon colony founded in 1853, and Fort Bridger were casualties of the federal invasion. Mormon leaders burned both when they heard troops were coming. A monument to Fort Supply stands today off County Road 279, near Robertson. Part of a Mormon wall remains at Fort Bridger.

Bridger leased the land where his trading post had stood to the U.S. Army. Judge W. A. Carter ran a trading mart at the military post and also raised cattle for military supply. He built up his herd by trading emigrants one healthy cow or ox for their two worn-out, emaciated ones. The town of Carter, north of I-80, is now nearly a ghost town.

Bridger spent the remainder of his active life guiding big game hunters and military troops searching for Indians hostile to pioneer emigrants. He couldn't read or write English, but

The homestead cabin of Elinore Pruitt Stewart, author of Letters from a Woman Homesteader *from which the movie* Heartland *was made, can be found southeast of Mountain View.*

he spoke the languages of several Indian tribes, knew sign languages, and often worked as interpreter.

The U.S. Army abandoned Fort Bridger in 1890. Land became available for homesteading then, and the town of Mountain View originated in 1891. Lyman was founded in the early 1900s as a Mormon colony.

Southeast of Mountain View, near Burntfork, is Elinore Pruitt Stewart's homestead. She wrote *Letters from a Woman Homesteader*, from which the movie *Heartland* was made.

Her letters to a former employer, first published in *Atlantic Monthly*, focused on her self-reliance and on the fun and camaraderie of homesteading, and called for other women to make a profitable life for themselves as she did. They are wonderful stories, mostly fictional. She married Clyde Stewart two weeks after filing on her land and signed her homestead over to her mother-in-law, who kept the land for four years, then sold it to Clyde Stewart for one hundred dollars.

The homestead still stands, but is off the road a mile or two and to visit it, you need permission from the current owner. Although Pruitt Stewart's stint as independent homesteader was short-lived, other Wyoming women did homestead successfully over a longer term. Nearly twelve per cent of Wyoming homesteaders were single women.

Burntfork is also the site of the first mountain man rendezvous, held in 1825.

During the 1970s Bridger Valley served as a bedroom community for workers at the oil and gas wells north of Evanston and the trona mines northwest of Green River. Houses were scarce, so mobile homes furnished most of the bedrooms. You can see the remains of one mobile home and trailer court, Scoop Shovel, on the north side of Interstate 80, just west of Fort Bridger.

When you leave Bridger Valley and head west toward Evanston you will drive over three steep hills, the bane of truck drivers. The polite name for these is "three sisters." Those poking fun at non-sexist language sometimes call them the "three siblings."

৵

*Answer: Thornburgh was a favorite dog of the soldiers at Fort Bridger. You can visit his grave at the fort.

Close-Up: CAROL AND RICHARD HAMILTON

CAROL HAMILTON'S GREAT-GRANDFATHER, Moses Byrne, built the Piedmont charcoal kilns. Richard's great-grandfather, Richard Henry Hamilton, was Judge Carter's full silent partner. The Hamiltons are a rarity in Wyoming in that they make their living solely from ranching.

You can visit the grave of Thornburgh at Fort Bridger. He was a favorite dog of the soldiers there.

"Ranching is probably the most liberating thing a woman can do," said Carol. "Except for a little height and muscle and leverage once in awhile, there's nothing I can't do as well as the hired man."

The Hamiltons run 550 head of cattle on their own land, on land they lease privately, and on land they lease from the Bureau of Land Management and the U.S. Forest Service. Their range runs from seven thousand to eleven thousand feet above sea level.

Some of the leases are mostly forest, Richard said, and will feed just six cows per section (six hundred forty acres) for three months. Some will feed eighteen cows per section. The Hamiltons have a rotation system so that the land isn't overgrazed. In winter they ship their calves to Los Olivos, California, to graze there; they have them shipped back to Wyoming in the spring.

Federal leases are essential to their livelihood, Richard said, because they can't count on enough private land to be continually available. "If I didn't lease, I would probably run forty per cent of the livestock I do now. One of us would be making a living and the other ranching."

But he said the government leasing fee isn't the bargain many people think it is. "I lease private pasture for ten dollars and fifty cents a month [per cow and calf]. On that private pasture they come and pick the cattle up about June first and deliver them in September. I provide no fencing, no minerals, no care, no doctoring. I don't even have to see the cattle.

"But it costs me fourteen dollars and seventy-two cents per cow-calf unit maintaining Forest Service land, and the cattle don't do as well as they do on private leases. Calves on private range are fifteen to twenty per cent heavier than they are on federal range. Our death loss is two to five per cent more on federal land. Part of them are stolen, some are poisoned. We don't have the control over poisonous plants that we do on private range.

"On the BLM and Forest Service land, it's ten miles to get there and another twenty-five to the top of the range. We provide all the fences, all the salt, we do all the doctoring. It's high labor-intensive. We average at least thirty miles a day in a pickup truck with a horse trailer or stock truck, over roads that are terrible.

"We're up there nearly every day so the cattle are not overgrazing, not on the road or along the river. One complaint from someone, and they're after us almost immediately. A lot of times the Forest Service will say, 'If we don't get any hassle, then you don't get any hassle.' It's sight management—if it looks nice, they don't worry about it."

"Environmentalists like to see land in a virginal state," said Carol. "They don't want it touched."

A private watchdog group has started an "Adopt an Allotment" program, in which members check to see that cattle are where they are supposed to be. So far any violations they have spotted on the Hamiltons' leases have been very minor, Richard said.

"When the public comes up to the mountains they want it to look nice," Carol said. "They don't want cow pies on their picnic ground; we get that complaint. A lot of times they don't realize they're picnicking on our private land! You can't tell what's private deeded land and what's government land.

"If something happened that there weren't deer anymore, the public would feel bad, because they like to look at them. But we would be even more sad, because we're experiencing this land; we have an emotional investment."

"Since legislation has been passed protecting wetlands and endangered species," Richard said, "we're saying 'Simon Says' all the time, making sure we don't step on anybody's toes with these acts."

"The idea behind these is incredibly good," said Carol. "We like wildlite. But you take a good idea, and by the time they give it to the bureaucracy, they blow it so out of shape that it's something the people can't live with. It's an oxymoron to say if we have more bureaucracy, we'll have improvement.

"We're overmanaged. Most of these things we have enough intelligence to do on our own. I don't think people realize the education and understanding and knowledge that it takes to manage a ranch. If you don't take care of the land, the land isn't going to take care of your cattle. If your cow doesn't eat right, she's not going to have a calf, and that's where the money is."

"We're into intense management," said Richard. "You have to manage to where you're weaning ninety-five per cent

People like Carol and Richard Hamilton are rare in Wyoming. They make their living solely from ranching.

of your calves, because otherwise you're not going to survive. In my dad's time, it was fifty per cent."

"We have the benefit of hindsight of the mistakes our grandparents made," said Carol. "If we made the same mistakes of overgrazing, we wouldn't be here."

"The general attitude of the public now is that cows don't belong on the land, and if the cow wasn't there, there'd be deer there; but the amount of wild game now is the highest in the history of the white man," Richard said. "My granddad never saw an elk, and he spent his entire life here. These last years the elk population has just exploded. Where there were one or two elk or deer or antelope, now there's one hundred fifty.

"We see sandhill cranes, raccoons, foxes, and game that were never here before. All of this wildlife has moved in with the cattle. We probably have more bio-diversity now than we've ever had.

"I have a vested interest in federal land, in dollars and in inheritance. My granddad's estate paid an inheritance tax on the [lease] permits. We bought our permits from my aunt and from my dad.

"Most of us ranchers have been here long enough so we've seen booms and busts. We're not the largest source of tax money—minerals are. But we're the steadiest amount of tax money. We've been here consistently."

"We're reasonable, we're responsible, we're stable," Carol said. "People know they can depend on us."

"People look at ranching from the romantic view of the past and don't realize the hard core of what it is now," Richard said. "We're running the same number of cattle now on our forest permits as in the forties, on three times the amount of land. It's so different from what my granddad did. He probably wouldn't like it now."

༈

Chapter 14

Evanston

EVANSTON, Wyoming's eighth largest town
Population 10,903   *Elevation 6,748*
*Question: What makes the Bear River unique?

Places to Visit
•• Bear River State Information Center. Turn off I-80 at East
Service Road. (A free RV dump site is also located here.)
•• Uinta County Museum in old Carnegie Library building, 36
Tenth Street. Chamber of Commerce is in the same building.
•• Almy Cemetery, off Highway 89 north of Evanston on
Almy Road, Route 107. Turn left (west) off Highway 89 at
Almy Fire Station, backtrack about one-half mile to cemetery.
•• Wyoming Downs, eight miles north on Highway 89.

A Brief Background
EVANSTON WAS FOUNDED IN 1868 and was named for Union
Pacific surveyor James Evans. The town's future was assured
when Union Pacific placed its roundhouse and machine
shops here.

Bear River City, eleven miles southeast, was Evanston's
rowdiest neighbor. When some railroad graders and tie-cut-
ters became too wild for townspeople to tolerate, roving publisher Leigh Freeman printed a warning in his *Frontier Index*

for all wrongdoers to "vacate the city or hang within sixty hours of this noon."

Five days later, three men robbed some Bear River citizens. The men were arrested and jailed. Vigilantes took them from the city jail and lynched them.

Friends and relatives of the dead men stormed the town, burned the jail, and destroyed the *Frontier Index* office with everything in it. Freeman fled Bear River City so fast, townsfolk said, "you could have played checkers on his coat-tails."

A battle between the vigilantes and rowdies ensued. Estimated casualty reports ranged from several who were severely wounded to forty-five or fifty dead. Bear River City became a ghost town after Union Pacific decided not to construct a siding to the main line at Evanston.

Almy, north of Evanston, was a coal mining town where a series of methane gas explosions killed many of the miners. In the Almy Cemetery you can find tombstones of men, some of them teenagers, who were killed in mine explosions in 1881, 1886 and 1895. The Union Pacific closed the mines in 1900.

During the nineteenth century Chinese coal miners, railroad workers, and small businessmen lived in Evanston. Evanston had one of only three Joss Houses (temples) in the United States. (The other two were in New York and San Francisco.) Pilgrims traveled hundreds of miles to visit the Joss House and observe Chinese New Year until Chinatown, and the Joss House, mysteriously burned in 1922.

Butch Cassidy once planned to rob a bank in Evanston, but a former Wild Bunch member alerted the bank owner, then warned Butch Cassidy that the banker was planning an ambush, so the robbery never happened.

In the Territorial session of 1886, legend has it that representatives were offered their choice of having the state university or the state mental hospital in Uinta County. They chose

In the Almy Cemetery you can find tombstones of men who were killed in mine explosions in 1881, 1886 and 1895.

the mental hospital, thinking that it would attract more permanent residents and help the economy more than the university would. (Some historians dispute this story.)

The hospital once housed as many as five hundred patients, who once grew their own food and worked in the hospital dairy. About 250 patients now reside there. The hospital is the old red brick building on a hill, visible from the Interstate.

Oil was discovered in Uinta County as early as 1832, but until the 1970s brought improved technology and the OPEC oil embargo, the cost of recovering the oil was too high to merit development. During the seventies the Overthrust Belt near

Evanston became a site of frenzied activity. Workers camped in the desert. Some lived in recreational vehicles in the hospital parking lot. T-shirts appeared reading "I was stuck in traffic in the Evanston underpass."

Today Evanston is a stable community with a semi-weekly newspaper, a spacious library, a civic orchestra and a community theatre. In the downtown area, modern government complexes stand next to buildings from the Victorian era.

～

*Answer: The Bear River is the longest river in this hemisphere that doesn't flow into an ocean. It begins in the Uinta Mountains, rambles five hundred miles through three states, and flows into the Great Salt Lake, ninety miles from its origin.

About The Close-Ups

•• Small towns offer as much to do as big cities, says Denice Wheeler. She makes herself happy and productive wherever she is, and for more than two decades she has lived in Evanston, Wyoming.

•• Running a race track in Wyoming has its advantages, says Joe Joyce. The native New Yorker previously worked at Madison Square Garden and was part-owner of Chicago's Arlington Track.

Close-Up: DENICE WHEELER

A LOT OF PEOPLE THINK DENICE Wheeler is a native of Evanston. She grew up in California, started college in Utah, married, had three children, divorced, went back to college, taught in public schools, owned and directed modeling and finishing schools, wrote poetry, raised her children, and did a self-improvement series on a Salt Lake City television show before moving to Evanston and marrying Joe Wheeler in 1968.

Denice Wheeler, who has lived in Evanston for more than twenty years, makes herself productive and happy wherever she is.

Since moving to Evanston she has been chairman of Wyoming's Commission on Women, president of Uinta County's Museum Board, chairman of Uinta County's U.S. Bicentennial and Wyoming Centennial committees, president of a University of Utah theatre group, president of Evanston's civic orchestra, and has been named Evanston's Businesswoman of the Year and Wyoming's Volunteer of the Year. Recently she was a delegate to the White House Conference on Libraries.

Until 1980 Wheeler helped manage the Jolly Roger Restaurant, which her late husband owned for thirty-four years. The Jolly Roger was once a part of Chinatown, and Wheeler has donated its collection of photographs to the county museum.

Wheeler's book *The Feminine Frontier: Wyoming Women 1850-1900* won the National Federation of Press Women award for the best historical research of 1989. She was co-author of the county museum's book *Facts and Fantasy of Uinta County's Past* and helped research and write *First Ladies of Wyoming*, a centennial project of the Wyoming Commission on Women.

"When I came to Evanston there were three thousand people here," Wheeler said. "This was such a bizarre change from Salt Lake City. When you come from out of state, you either hate it or you love it."

Wheeler loves Evanston, Wyoming. She even likes Wyoming winters. One way to enjoy living in Wyoming, she said, is to get involved in sports.

"The very first thing I did here was start cross-country skiing. We have fantastic trails thirty minutes from here, in the high Uintas.

"I was one of the first to go to Yellowstone when they opened it up to snowmobiling. We have ice skating on the reservoir for a month every winter. And I play racquetball all winter, indoors. I don't play in the summer because I'd rather be outdoors.

"I've been all over the world, and I'm totally happy here," said Wheeler. "I just think there's more fun in a small town. The thing that I sense here more than anything else is one never needs be an isolate. There's no excuse for not being involved because there's so much work to do. I got very involved in history—taking photographs of historical sites, doing oral histories...."

Wheeler calls herself an amateur historian. For twelve years she wrote a historical column for the *Salt Lake City Tribune*. For five years she hosted a radio show in Evanston, *Our Pioneer Heritage*, which won a Wyoming State historical award.

"The diversity of our history is what makes it so incredible. We had the mountain men, the ranchers, the railroad, the pioneer homesteaders, coal miners, oil and gas companies, charcoal kilns.... Almost everything that happened in the West happened in Uinta County. You can learn about the military era at Fort Bridger, the Indian era, bootlegging, prostitution, gambling—it was all here."

During the summers Wheeler leads foreign visitors on tours of the West. "When they come here, they're just incredulous. They expect cowboys and Indians and the excitement of the wilds and the animals. It's the romantic Western history that people can relate to, distorted as it is. There's no place in the world, I think, that has as many mountain men rendezvous today as we do in Wyoming.

"I think another reason people have an interest in Wyoming history—it feels like yesterday. I've had people accuse me of talking as if I knew those people of the 1860s and 1870s. I feel as though I do."

Lately Wheeler doesn't spend much time in Evanston. After her husband died she became spokesperson for Women's Initiative, a program sponsored by the American Association of Retired Persons. From January to May she gives lectures and classes on problems facing women. She travels continually throughout the United States.

"I gave forty-two talks this year in Wyoming alone. People say, 'How can you travel alone?' I don't feel alone in Wyoming. Our governor [Mike Sullivan] has said, 'Wyoming's my home town.' I could go anywhere in Wyoming and stay overnight with someone or meet somebody for lunch or dinner. I'm never far from someone I know.

"If you walk down any street in Wyoming and you say hello, people will say, 'Hi, how are you?' When I travel out of state, I put Wyoming decals on my rental cars, because I want people to know I'm from Wyoming. I'm proud of it."

Wheeler doesn't seek controversy, but she doesn't run away from it, either. When a seniors group invited her to come and give a lecture, then walked around and visited with each other while she was speaking, she told them to sit down and shut up, that she wasn't going to put up with such rudeness.

"I didn't put up with that kind of nonsense when I was teaching and I wasn't going to now. I was one tough mother. Actually, they were really sweet afterwards, when I just talked to them one-on-one. I don't think they even realized they were being rude."

Wheeler made Cable Network News in 1991, when she chaired a ten-state women's conference and censored a conference art exhibit.

Said Wheeler: "It was *my* cocktail party, in *my* room, in *my* hotel. It wasn't a public function. I was very careful with my language. I didn't say the paintings were obscene or pornographic, I just said they were inappropriate. The press was there immediately, so I'm sure I was being set up."

Two of Wheeler's grown children live in Evanston now, although they were raised in Utah and have lived in several other states. "I'm involved in an awful lot here," Wheeler said. "In Evanston I have family and friendship and community involvement and outdoor sports. I like coming home to Evanston. But I'm just as comfortable in any Wyoming town."

Close-Up: WYOMING DOWNS

Wyoming Downs is Wyoming's only privately-owned race track, open Saturdays, Sundays and holidays Memorial day through Labor Day. Races begin at one P.M. and run until six or six thirty P.M. (twelve or thirteen races per day). General admission is three dollars.

Wyoming Downs has a seven-eighths mile track and races thoroughbreds and quarter horses.

Managing Wyoming Downs is a far cry from Joe Joyce's previous enterprises. The native New Yorker practiced law for seventeen years, was associated with New York's Madison Square Garden, and was part-owner/manager of Chicago's Arlington Track for fourteen years before buying Wyoming Downs in 1989.

"In a lot of ways this is better [than operating a big-city race track]," Joyce said. "People know a lot more about horses out here. We get a lot of people who come just to watch the horses run, without betting on them.

"There's a strong work ethic here—people put in a good day's work for their wages. And I sure don't miss city traffic."

Wyoming Downs is out in the country, with a backdrop of rangeland and mountains. The racetrack encircles a clear blue pond.

The track offers pari-mutuel wagering. "You don't bet against the house, you bet against each other," Joyce said.

Native New Yorker Joe Joyce thinks running a race track in Wyoming has its advantages.

Eighty per cent of the money wagered goes back to the betters, in accordance with state regulations. Percentages vary according to the type of bet. The minimum bet is two dollars, the same as it was in 1922.

The Downs has a seven-eighths mile track and races thoroughbreds and quarter horses. Most of the quarter horses come from Utah, while the thoroughbreds come from all the western states, including Wyoming.

Joyce estimates that the Downs brings three thousand to four thousand people into Evanston every weekend it is open. Most of them come from Utah. Some arrive on tour buses. Many people bring small children and set up folding chairs next to the track.

"It's a family-oriented crowd here—a much younger crowd than goes to most racetracks. From that standpoint it's nice—it's refreshing," Joyce said.

Joyce employs 240 people, in addition to the trainers and jockeys individual owners bring in. "This place has the largest impact on Uinta County of any single enterprise," he said. "Our economic impact on the county is probably ten million dollars." His greatest profit margin comes from selling concessions, he said, not from wagering.

Year-round off-track betting in several Wyoming towns subsidizes Wyoming Downs. That's the only way a small racetrack can survive, Joyce said. Off-track wagerers watch races live by satellite from California, Louisiana, and New Mexico tracks.

At Wyoming Downs, some betters come early to watch videos of the previous weekend's races. Some pore over racing forms just as business investors study the stock market. Others bet by their lucky numbers or by the standings of jockeys and trainers listed in the program.

"The thing about horse racing and wagering, it's very cerebral," Joyce said. "A lot of professional people bet at the races. It's competitive, putting your judgment up above everyone else's. All you have to do is be twenty per cent smarter than everyone else and you're going to win.

"It's kind of fun. Obviously, I like it."

ᠵᡃ

Chapter 15
Leaving Wyoming

You have just a few miles left to travel to the Wyoming-Utah border. I hope you enjoyed your trip across southern Wyoming and that you will remember some of the people who live and work there.

From now on, if anyone traveling across Wyoming via Interstate 80 tells you, "There's nothing there"—you will know better.

✧

About the Author

MARY ANN TREVATHAN GREW UP in New York State, attended college in Pennsylvania, then headed west to teach English in a small Wyoming high school. She married a Virginian, lived in Wyoming eight years, and still spends most summers there. She lives now in Morro Bay, California, where she writes freelance articles for magazines and newspapers. She is currently researching a book on California's Imperial Valley.

This book was printed on 55-pound Huron Natural acid-free, recycled paper.